Emergence:

Memories from a Journey into the Light

Emergence:
Memories from a Journey into the Light

Ann Fieldhouse

ATHENA PRESS
LONDON

Emergence:
Memories from a Journey into the Light
Copyright © Ann Fieldhouse 2010

All Rights Reserved

No part of this book may be reproduced in any form
by photocopying or by any electronic or mechanical means,
including information storage or retrieval systems,
without permission in writing from both the copyright
owner and the publisher of this book.

ISBN 978 1 84748 787 2

First published 2010 by
ATHENA PRESS
Queen's House, 2 Holly Road
Twickenham TW1 4EG
United Kingdom

Printed for Athena Press

For my children

Contents

INTRODUCTION	9
1. THE EARLY YEARS	10
Childhood	10
Adolescence	16
A Young Adult	23
My Mother	26
Becoming a Mother	32
Relationship Breakdown	35
2. THE MIDDLE YEARS	42
Becoming Aware	42
The Body	*43*
The Mind	*47*
The Emotions	*48*
Recovering the Inner Child	53
Empowerment	60
Codependency	67
Searching for Answers	71
Connecting with Planet Earth	79
My Path	86

3. THE LATER YEARS	96
Looking Back	96
Remembering Those I Met Along the Way	102
Opening to the Light	115
Soul-presence on Earth	125
POSTSCRIPT: ONE YEAR LATER	132

Introduction

In my twenties, I started to write what I called my 'poems', and at different times since I have returned to this form of expression. They were written to describe a memory, more often to exorcise a strong emotion or to try and make sense of what was happening to me or arising in me. In later years it was to express the wonder of a new awareness that was arising in me and to express the beauty of seeing the world through new eyes. 'Always worthwhile, a bit of poetry,' someone once said to me. It has certainly been worthwhile for me, as over the years it has allowed me to express myself, even if it was only to myself, in a way I could not when I was younger.

I conceived the idea of putting them all together in a chronological order to trace my progress, to highlight how that expression had changed. Then I started to write a line to describe why I wrote each piece of writing (I find myself hesitating to call them 'poems' now) and before I knew it, those descriptions were taking over and a lot of memories came pouring out. It has turned into a memoir, snippets from different times in my life, giving a flavour of what I was feeling at the time. It has turned into a chart of my emergence into the light of awareness from the dark tunnel I inhabited at the beginning of my life. It is my emergence from the dark depressions, emptiness and hopelessness of my early years into the calm waters of awareness, the joy of living and a serenity of being.

1. The Early Years

CHILDHOOD

I was brought up in Flixton which is at the end of the bus line out from Manchester and then a half-mile walk down the road to a huddle of houses surrounded by farmland (as it was then – it's more built-up now.) There was a train track on the horizon that rose higher and higher to go over the canal bridge. This was the Manchester Ship Canal, so the bridge had to be high enough for ocean-going ships to pass through. I have memories of watching ships looming out of the mist, sailing through the fields – or so it looked. Some of them were large enough to tower over the houses, and these mighty vessels needed tugs to pilot them through the canal. The locks were consequently very large and very deep. When we needed to cross the canal (to visit the vet on the other side) the ferryman would take us in a wooden boat with a single scull. The canal seemed very wide especially when we were in that ferryboat in the middle of the crossing, watching a huge liner coming out of the locks towards us. The water was also very oily, so that when our dog fell in once (she missed her footing jumping down into the boat), it took several shampoos to get her clean.

I have some good memories of playing out with the other children, which I did until the age of eleven. Our house looked over farm fields, which spread out until they reached the canal and the railway. We had what we called a pasture field in which to play, with its own stream to paddle in and catch tiddlers (and put them back), a hill to roll down, trees to climb, bushes to make caves in, brambles to eat blackberries from, and marshy patches to jump over. We didn't return home till we were hungry, dirty and happy. Looking back, those summers were quite idyllic. The fields were ploughed by Jimmy, the farm worker, and two Shire horses, the gulls screeching and wheeling around behind them. In the late summer he would scythe round the edges of the field before the horses pulled the wooden harvester, gathering in the wheat, oats or barley. We were always there watching, playing, getting in his way. He had a very earthy turn of phrase. (In later years, the horses were replaced by a tractor, and then one summer there appeared a shiny red combine harvester. Oh, the wonder!)

We weren't allowed near the canal on our own because one of the boys of my mother's generation had fallen in and drowned. He was a good swimmer but had hit his head on the side of the lock as he fell. My mother, who had lived in the house since she was ten years old, was taken with all the other children to see his dead body as a warning against going near the canal. She remembered how white and bloated he looked; she was probably about eleven by then. The fear and dread instilled in her and the other children on that day were passed on to us – the next generation.

GOING OUT TO PLAY

Sunlight and laughter,
Playing in the fields

We went around together –
All ages, boys and girls –

Fell out, made up,
Tumbled down the hill,

Climbed the well-worn tree,
Boys always one branch higher than the girls,

Watched Jimmy with his scythe
Before the harvester reaped around

And then the coupled working horses
Ploughed furrows in the ground.

Taboo made mystery of the canal –
Locks visited only with a grown-up,

> Small stabs of fear
> As we gazed into the water;
>
> Suppose we fell in –
> What would it feel like as we slowly went under?

There is one memory outside the home during this period, which was not so pleasant. Not everything was idyllic playing out. There were the occasions when I would get told off by one of the mothers or fall out with another child. Aged about five and playing in our pasture field, we hit on the brilliant idea of taking off our clothes. Innocently prancing around, one of the older boys came into the field, saw us, turned red and immediately ran off. Next one of the mothers came. She told us off, got us dressed and turned to me saying, 'I'm surprised at you, Ann, you should have known better!' This puzzled me, because I was only three months older than her son, so why would I know better than him and about what? I am still puzzled. Anyway, we were made to feel we had done something wrong.

A few days later there were a few of us playing in a boy's garden. Unusually for those days, his mother was a single mum who also looked after her physically disabled brother – he had a hunchback and a 'hunch front', as I called it then. This afternoon he called me into the hen house and locked the door. My next memory is of lying on my back with no clothes on while he held a hand mirror so that I could see myself and lectured me on not allowing boys to touch me down there as it was very precious. He had heard about our taking off our clothes. I tried to get up but he was holding me down and I could not move. That is the feeling that is the strongest, this not being able to move, not being able to escape. I was frozen inside. I think I was told not to tell anyone.

My next memory is of being outside and looking around at the other children to see if they had noticed anything, hoping they had not. I never told anyone. In fact I did not remember it as an adult until I did a 'women and sexuality' course many years later. When I was about thirteen I was walking past the same man on my way home from school. Wheelchair-bound by now, he was sitting outside his house watching the world go by. I looked over at him and couldn't bear the knowing way he was looking at me. From then on I used to go a different way so as to avoid him. For many years I found it difficult seeing men with a physical disability.

A couple of years later, I was in the front room of one of the children's houses. Their blind uncle had come to visit. He was left alone with us two girls and decided he wanted to give us a kiss. He caught hold of me and hauled me over his knees, but I was face down so I struggled to right myself. Again the memory is of not being able to move, these strong arms pinning me down no matter how much I struggled, knowing that physically there was nothing I could do to get away. I blurted out, 'I'm the wrong way up!' and he allowed me to turn over within the circle of his arms and proceeded to give me the 'big kiss' on the lips. I stayed away from him for the remainder of the visit.

Interestingly, these are the only two memories I have of male touch as a child. My father never touched me – no pat on the back, ruffle of hair, sitting on his knee, putting on socks. Touch and the warmth of that form of connection came from my mother.

One further memory of outside the house was when a group of us children were walking to Sunday school. I was carrying a beret and swung it at one of the boys because he was teasing me – I didn't take too kindly to boys teasing me in those days. I thought no more of it, and we had walked a good half a mile when I received a hard bang on the head which really hurt. The boy had hit me over the head with a large stick. Crying in shock and pain, I ran back home. My mother stormed round next door to the boy's mother and complained loudly. An hour or so later the other mother stormed round to us with her son to show a mark on her son's forehead where the brooch on my beret had scratched him. I hadn't realised that had happened. None of us spoke to each other for years, neither the mothers nor us children. (I include this memory because… well, later!)

Although I have some wonderful summer memories of being outside, I have very few memories of being inside the house before the age of eleven. My father and great-grandmother were cold, rigid, disapproving people. I was an only child and we lived in my great-grandmother's house. She was seventy when I was born and required that I be quiet; quite a feat for my mother, trying to keep a small child from making any noise. My great-grandmother had brought up my mother (her granddaughter) from the age of two years when my mother's parents divorced and did not want to or could not keep the two children. This was back in 1921. Her father went back to Ireland. My mother's younger sister, Patricia, was placed in a home until she was adopted some years later. They were never able to trace her again. My mother's mother was quite a character, by all accounts. Outgoing and living life to the full, she sounds as though she went her own way. She drove a taxi during the Second World War – the first woman in Manchester to do so, or so I was told. Her younger brother, Hubert, signed up to fight in the First World War and was killed aged eighteen. My mother (and then I) grew up with his extremely large picture on the wall in his army uniform, together with the citation received on his death.

I have one memory of being about eight years old and coming back home late from visiting a friend. One of the reasons I was late is because she told me that in a house I had to walk by there lived a witch who preyed on little girls. It took a long while for me to pluck up the courage to run past that house! When I arrived home, my mother opened the living-room door to see where I had been. I refused to go into the room and stayed in the hall, because I thought my father was sitting in there and couldn't bear the thought of him seeing me. She stood in the doorway telling me off, and I was trying to look through the crack to see what he was doing when I heard a door open and realised that my father was coming into the hall behind me. I'd got it wrong! My mind blanked off at that moment. I realise now that I was afraid of my father.

Another incident around this time was my mother going out to the cinema on her own, leaving me with my father and great-grandmother. The memory is so vivid that I know she was going to see her favourite actor, Jack Hawkins, in *The Cruel Sea*. She never went out in the evenings, and I began to make a huge fuss about wanting to go with her, whining, pleading, crying, while she gave me ever increasing amounts of sweets and chocolate bars to try and pacify me. Eventually she went, and I was left in the living room sitting at the table strewn with all these sweets. Disgusted with me, my father told me off and took away all the sweets. My final memory is looking over at the cold and disapproving figures of my great-grandmother sitting on one side of the fire and my father the other. My outburst was out of character. I had never behaved like that before. Again, I realise in hindsight that I hadn't wanted to be left alone with these two silent, forbidding adults.

When I was eleven years old I became aware that my parents would begin arguing as soon as I was in bed. It was my father's voice that I heard. He would shout very loudly and violently, an ugly, threatening sound. He would also throw, bang and smash whatever he could get his hands on: the furniture or his pudding (with custard – it remained stuck on the ceiling for years). He only ever did this when I was in bed, supposedly asleep, because he thought he was protecting me. When I did hear him, I couldn't bear it and I hid under the pillow, pulling it around my ears to blot out the sound. For years I could never understand why I had had such a strong reaction. I have since learned that up to puberty we tend to absorb everything inwards, but when puberty hits our consciousness begins to extend outwards, which means my reaction was extreme because I had heard this before but had been blanking it out of my consciousness. What I was experiencing at eleven and onwards was what I had felt at an earlier age. At the age of eleven, though, I had no awareness that it had happened before.

Looking back, I realise that hearing my father's rage could have been one of the reasons I had suddenly developed a fear of heights. I remember climbing those high trees in our pasture field with no hesitation at all. I remember in my first year at grammar school I had no qualms about climbing the ropes in the gym, or rolling over bars. Suddenly I couldn't do any of this. The ground had been taken away from under my feet. I had a fear of falling. I found it difficult even to walk over a slatted bridge just a foot above the water. I could feel myself falling into the black depths…

Although it's not actually a memory, my mother told me later that as a baby my cries were not answered. She said that from the age of two weeks, which was when my mother brought me back from the cottage hospital, my father prevented her coming to me once I was put to bed at night. His belief was that all babies try it on, and leave me alone long enough and I would stop. Of course, I stopped. I just gave up trying to get my needs met, a pattern I have struggled with for much of my life.

I had a recurring nightmare during these years. It was as though the moon was hanging over me. To start it was smooth – semolina smooth – but it was so close I could only see part of it as it moved nearer and nearer to me. Then the surface would change into dark, jagged craters. Both surfaces filled me with terror as they inexorably moved to smother me, but it was the semolina-smooth surface that was the most frightening.

ADOLESCENCE

From around the age of eleven I stopped playing out, became more and more withdrawn and was very depressed and unhappy throughout my teens. Often I have said (dramatically) that they were the worst years of my life. It did seem towards the end we were all living a nightmare. Looking back it was a very dark period in my existence.

When I was five, my great-grandmother became an invalid, took to her bed, which was in the front room downstairs, and stayed there till she died ten years later. My mother was forced into the role of carer, having been made aware for most of her life of how much she owed her grandmother for taking her in. She was deeply unhappy and when I was about twelve years old started to become increasingly dependant on me emotionally. Unfulfilled, despairing, angry and depressed she blamed my father, her real mother and the burden of nursing her grandmother for the drudgery of her life. She cried on my shoulder, an emotional outpouring that overwhelmed me. At the same time she took her anger and rage out on me as well as my father. Saying or doing the wrong thing would result in emotional withdrawal – heavy, dark, raw silences – as she punished me for 'hurting' her or for 'not loving her enough'. Or it could result in a prolonged tirade about all my shortcomings, the biggest of which was how I failed as a daughter, followed by how like my father I was (and we all knew how lacking he was) – in other words, I was just not good enough.

I have a memory of being in the classroom at school, aged about fourteen, waiting for the lesson to start. I was talking happily to some girls when suddenly I found myself banging on the desk and shouting, then bursting into tears and sobbing and sobbing for the rest of the lesson. I had no idea why I broke down like this, because again it was out of character. I was usually very contained and controlled during those years. No one was to know what was going on inside me or in my home life. *I* didn't know what was going on inside me.

Again in the classroom, we were having a French lesson when the teacher started to tell me off. I don't know what I had been doing. Maybe I had talked to the girl I was sitting next to; nothing to warrant what came next. It turned into a harangue. She went on and on detailing all the things wrong with me. She seemed to be enjoying it. I was not the first girl she had done this to. Stony-faced, I was trying to stop the tears in my eyes from falling. It seemed very important to not show it was getting to me. After lunch she came into the classroom again and singled me out to be very nice to. She was obviously regretting going as far as she had. These harangues, these tirades were following me – at home and now at school.

Another memory of this time is that I hated being looked at. One hot summer I went around in a cardigan with long sleeves because I didn't want anyone to see my bare arms. I needed to hide behind my clothes. It didn't help that a 'helpful' friend had relayed to me that a boy was not interested in me because I was 'too tall and too shy'. I had shot up in my early teens and towered over my age group. I was what was known as 'lanky', with thin, straight, mouse-coloured hair. My mother and great-grandmother had very long, thick hair, grey eyes and strong features. I took after my brown-eyed, bald father. I have always longed for beautiful, long, thick wavy hair. My daughter has it but it missed me by. I was also incredibly self-conscious and yes, I was painfully shy.

My mother took me with her to Strangeways Prison, as she had an appointment to discuss her marriage problems with someone there. (Why the prison? I have no idea.) I was in the room with my mother and the 'counsellor' all the time, and at one point the counsellor asked me what I thought was the reason for all these difficulties between my parents. I felt resentful at having to answer. I didn't want to talk. Why was the counsellor not insisting on seeing my mother on her own? I didn't want to be there. I was only about fourteen at the time yet, ever dutiful, I muttered something about it being difficult because of having to look after my great-grandmother. Anything I did know was what my mother had told me.

This next piece of writing is a memory of when, aged sixteen, I accompanied my mother as her 'responsible adult' for her to have electric shock treatment. She was suffering from depression (later diagnosed as 'manic depression', as it was then called). However, she would not tell my father about this treatment because he refused to accept she had any problems. I did once try to tell him she was ill but he said she had always been like that: 'bad-tempered and bloody-minded'. I have two memories, the first sitting in the waiting room, and then standing at the bus stop afterwards holding my mother, who was very dazed (it affects the memory in the short term) and was leaning on me.

Memory

>Across to the other side of town
>To a place of no name, dark and unfamiliar,
>Only dimly aware of why we were going
>Not really understanding what was to happen.
>
>How old were we? I've never thought.
>How were we dressed – what did we say?
>Memories gone.
>
>Except for the waiting room, people seated around,
>Packed in, overcrowded
>Lined faces, pale, dull, closed in.

While I waited, I looked around.
Who were the prospective patients – who the relatives, friends?
We all looked alike, each locked away inside,
No laughter, hurried whispers, apprehension:

Would a patient erupt out of his inner torment,
Filling the room with frightening tension?
Would a relative break down under the strain, weeping for a loved one?
Who were the real patients, who in most need? Any of us – all of us?

My name called out, the treatment over,
The 'patient' handed into my charge.
We stood at the bus stop; she didn't know where she was,
Her memory tampered with, dazed, leaning on me.

We stood at the bus stop, the other side of town,
Everywhere strange and I couldn't remember
Which bus we had to catch...

Being very empathic, I lived her nightmare with her and was desperate to make it better for her. Our doctor told her that she should live her life vicariously through me. With tears streaming down my face I promised her she could. I would make it all right for her. A neighbour once told me not to take sides. Sullen and resentful, I couldn't reply. It was none of her business. She shouldn't be talking to me about this. I didn't want anyone else knowing what was going on, but more than that she just did not understand. What choice did I have but to support my mother? She needed my support, she had been so badly treated all her life, she had no one else to turn to (so she told me) and so on... I was overwhelmed by her unhappiness and depression.

Such was their relationship that when I was seventeen my parents separated but stayed under the same roof. (There was insufficient money for one or the other to move out, plus they were far too codependent.) My mother and I were living, eating and sleeping in one room downstairs with my father in the other room, and war broke out every time they met. I have a memory of them running side by side down the hall to the bathroom (it was downstairs), jostling each other out of the way as they tried to beat the other to get there first, all the while calling each other names. I turned away quickly not able to watch. In that moment, it seemed I was the adult and they were the children.

I can't remember why I was not in my own bedroom upstairs. I think it was being decorated, but my father downed tools for some reason. For years my father refused to decorate because my mother refused to clean because he refused to decorate because she... and so it went on. I remember the walls in the kitchen, full of grease, blackened with dust and cobwebs. I couldn't bear the thought of anyone else seeing it.

In my late teens, while returning home from school or work, I was aware of a sinking feeling inside, my footsteps slowing and a growing sense of dread, because I never knew whether I would be met with a friendly welcome, angry words, or silence with a note on the table saying my dinner was in the oven. All this while we sat in the same room together. If it was the silence, then a few days would go by until I would find a note on the table again saying, 'Let's be friends,' and I would feel such relief. Connection was re-established.

I did ask my father at one point if he would finish my bedroom so that I could go back to sleep there. I was feeling trapped, having nowhere to go for respite. I was also ashamed of having to sleep in the same bed as my mother. However, I was reading in bed one Saturday morning when he thought I should have been up, and he refused to continue. My mother was out at the time or he would not have come into the room. So 'trapped' I remained.

During my last year at home I started to answer back when my mother threw her anger at me. At least I think I did, because I have just one memory of screaming and throwing a clock at her. It missed, but this was not how I had been for most of my teens. I have memories of just sitting there while she lashed out at me, keeping it all in, trying not to allow anything to show. It was as if to show what I was feeling would be dangerous. So successful was I that often she accused me of being indifferent and uncaring – 'just like your father!' It's possible that during this last year her influence had started to wane, as I was forming a relationship with my husband-to-be. Part of the basis for this relationship was that I found it incredibly easy to talk to him, something I had not been able to do up till then with anyone.

I don't think my father hit my mother, although I did see him do so once. It was not much of a hit – she wasn't hurt. Neither could I blame him too much, because my mother had said some awful things to him about his sexuality, and it was in front of me. (She had a truly vicious tongue at times.) He would have been mortified that these things were revealed to me; he was such a private man and also had real issues about sex. Yes, my mother told me all! He threw her out of the room and locked the door with me inside. I stomped out after her (I still couldn't be alone with my father) and really told her off. It might have been the time I threw the clock at her!

The Christmas before I left home it didn't seem fair that my father should be alone on that day, and I insisted that I would have my dinner with my mother and my tea with him. I even made a Christmas tree for him. The meal with him was difficult. We had nothing to talk about. We were not used to talking to each other. In his presence I would freeze up and my mind would go blank. I wonder if it was the same for him.

To be the centre of attention was anathema for me. Looking back, I know that I survived by being on the outside of my primary group – my family. I have an image of me aged about six sitting on an ottoman under the window. The curtains are drawn because it's an early winter's evening. The room is quite dark, just the glow from the fire. I am looking at the three grown-ups sitting around the open fire, my father's back to me, my mother opposite him, my great-grandmother sideways on. They are not talking; all of them are looking at the fire, all of them turned inwards. I am on the outside. It's safe to be there – lonely, unloved but safe. *I need to be quiet so they forget I'm here.* I am not sure whether that's a real memory or not, but it's an image I have frequently that seems to represent how I existed in those early years.

So when, as a prefect in the sixth form, I had to sit on the platform in the school hall alongside the headmistress to give the Bible reading and say the prayer in front of 700 girls and teachers, can you imagine the nightmares beforehand? I delayed going on to the platform for so long a teacher had to come to find me to say that the headmistress was waiting, as she was the one who came last when everyone was in place. I walked down the aisle in front of all these people onto the platform, only to find the huge Bible had not been opened to the page I needed. I remember all those eyes on me. I was absolutely frozen inside. My face felt wooden. My movements felt stiff and clumsy. (So much did I fear being the centre of attention that I never had dreams of a white wedding. Both my marriages have been in registry offices, with just one or two people present as witnesses.)

One piece of brightness during these teen years was that I had a school friend, Anne, and in the earlier years we visited each other's houses (before things began to get out of hand in my own home). I enjoyed being in her house. It was warm, and her parents would sit in the same chair, obviously happy to be together. Her father was warm and fun-loving. She was the eldest of two brothers and a sister. It felt like a real home. But even with Anne there was no question of confiding what was going on. I didn't understand what was happening.

When I was eighteen, I was away from home for two months as an au pair in France looking after a newborn baby. I was living just outside Paris and every morning attended the Sorbonne for a 'French for foreigners' course. There were many different nationalities and the common language, of course, was French. In particular I remember a young English priest who spoke near-perfect French but with a strong Yorkshire accent (he was going out to a French part of Africa to be a missionary). I sat next to him and felt safe. Looking back, it was an interesting six weeks, although I was still frozen inside, very self-conscious and couldn't feel the experience at the time, even when I was dancing in the streets on Bastille Day.

I felt I had to pretend all the time – pretending I was having a good time, pretending I was full of that aliveness that others seemed to have. It was as though it was all happening to someone else. I remember feeling very homesick and had a yearning for suet pudding. I had my mother send me the ingredients but I couldn't get it to rise. I remember being very upset at seeing a bear on a chain having to dance to the music from an old-fashioned barrel organ being pushed through the streets, with a monkey also on a chain having to pull stops and things. It seemed so cruel. The consensus of the class was that my reaction was typically English, as the English were far too sentimental over animals.

When I got back home I was visited by a school friend who wanted to make arrangements with me about starting secretarial college together. She said she had imagined I'd have looked different from being in Paris, but it didn't seem to have rubbed off on me. It hadn't touched me in any way, inside or out.

A Young Adult

Is it taught or is it innate? Like my mother, I was subject to depression and I did not seem to have any control of my moods. I was shy, quiet, introverted, lacked confidence and depressed. In those years I probably came across as aloof and cold, at times sharp and prickly, protecting myself by giving out little. Turned in on myself, I was afraid to trust anyone. I envied those with warm, open, friendly dispositions. They were in the centre of any group because people naturally responded to them, liked them and enjoyed being with them. I remained on the boundary, miserably looking on, wishing I could be different, not liking myself, not feeling good enough. Inwardly I was afraid to let anybody see me, because then they would really find me out as unworthy.

Depression

> The cloud descends slowly, slowly,
> Warning feathers of thought flutter aimlessly around.
> The light wanes weakly, feebly,
> Troubling pangs of worry close in, without sound.
> Darkness gathers broodingly, broodingly,
> Barbs of fear throb relentlessly, hate and pain abound.
> The light fades finally, totally,
> Darkness, suffocating, swirls blackly round and
>   round.

By now newly married and living in London, I worked as a secretary during the day while my husband set up his own engineering business, for which I did all the bookkeeping and secretarial work in the evenings. We worked closely. We didn't socialise much. We depended solely on each other. We were very codependent.

For years I did not know what my reality was. Was it when I was feeling high or when I was feeling low? It's as if the whole world changed. (It wasn't until much later that I learned that neither was real, that there was a third reality of balance and clear seeing.) When I was high, everything was possible for those few moments. However, much of this time I struggled with dark depressions, struggled with work, struggled relating to the people there… just simply struggled.

The Greyness of Life

> I cannot remember being born,
> Yet cannot forget the years since worn.
> I cannot admit to growing old,
> Yet cannot retrieve that youth so bold.
>
> How can I remedy a living
> That was so wasted, so full of nothing?
> How can I lift the burden of memory,
> The weight of selfish, worthless reverie?
>
> I fear the greyness of Life within me
> Yet know not how to treat it.
> I feel the blackness of Death before me,
> Yet know not how to greet it.

During my twenties, I did not have friends outside work. I would go to work and occasionally would meet someone I could get on with, enjoying working with them; but outside work I couldn't relax with them. On the very few occasions I went to their homes, I would be ill at ease, frozen inside, my mind a blank. I could relate to them at work, where I had a role to hide behind, but outside I could not join in. Even when I had my first child I still didn't know anyone, and my baby was eighteen months old before I left her with anyone. I was eight months pregnant again and needed to attend a hospital appointment; a neighbour offered. It wasn't until about a year or so after the birth of my second child that, in desperation and feeling completely isolated, I wrote to the local church for help and joined my first mother and toddler group. During these times I was at home during the day, not knowing anyone, looking out of the window at the world outside.

IMPRISONED

A life sentence has been passed
And a Spirit chafes in solitary confinement,
Hemmed in by darkly smothering walls,
Made tall and close by rigid convention.

A life sentence is the punishment
Befitting the crime of youth's impulsiveness,
Condemned to forced labour in a daily routine,
Under constant surveillance of boredom and loneliness.

The World's outside, waiting, welcoming,
Pulsating its message of life and freedom
And a yearning Spirit looks out
And weeps in frustration and hopelessness,
As the gates of conscience refuse to yield.

A life sentence is to be served
And a Spirit sobs for all it has lost
Imprisoned within those unflinching walls,
The four walls of my mind.

I did not transplant easily. I did not feel I belonged in London. What were familiar had been my home in Flixton and the fields around. Often I thought, *What on earth am I doing around here?* It seemed so unfriendly, so impersonal compared to the North. It took me many years to overcome these feelings of isolation, disconnection and alienation from everything around me.

My Mother

When my great-grandmother died (I was fifteen), my mother's depression became much worse, and for the next ten years she took quite a few overdoses – many of them because we did not love her enough, or so she told me. When she started it was a crime to attempt suicide, but our doctor would never report her and wrote it up as influenza.

The first time she did this I had arrived back in London from an exchange visit to France. While there I had received a very black letter from my mother which had really depressed me. I remember this because the mother of the family I was staying with was really nice to me afterwards, even though she didn't know what the matter was. When I arrived back in London I was met by my father, and as we were walking from the rail to the coach station, he told me that the reason my mother had not come was because she had taken an overdose and was in bed recovering.

I remember another occasion when she told me (not my father, he mustn't know) that she had taken the rest of her tablets, and would I take her to the doctor. We walked the fifteen minutes to the bus stop, waited for the bus, took the twenty-minute ride to the doctor and waited in the waiting room until she was called. Then we went in to the doctor, where she turned from my usual acerbic, straight-talking mother into a whining little girl who 'didn't know what to do'. She was told off by the doctor and told to go home to sleep it off. Immediately on leaving the surgery, she reverted to her usual self with the words, 'Well, that was a waste of time!'

We then waited at the bus stop, took the twenty-minute bus journey back and walked the fifteen-minute route back home, during which she was now so dopey and tired she was literally slumped on me as we walked along. I was dreading meeting up with any of the neighbours.

There was only one time I remember my mother talking to

anyone else about her problems (save the professionals), and that was to the neighbour who had told me not to choose sides. The three of us were sitting in our back room. My mother was saying quite calmly she would 'end it all' and that she had enough pills saved up. While she was talking, she kept rubbing her hand up and down her leg from knee to ankle, over and over again, leaning right down each time then back up. It began to look as if she were mentally disturbed. I could see the neighbour looking at her and getting worried. Just as with the doctor, she had changed her personality in front of this neighbour. For a moment a part of me separated and watched my mother 'play-acting', putting on a good show for the neighbour. As soon as the neighbour went, she was back to her normal self.

For five years I had shouldered the burden of her depressions because my father did not believe she was 'ill'. After I left home, it was my father's turn to shoulder them. He could no longer ignore them. I was visiting them one weekend and was just about to leave when he took me aside and explained how my mother's behaviour was becoming very strange and obsessive. For example, she would wrap each single piece of cutlery in a cloth, followed by several rounds of plastic, and finally tie them up tightly. He told me he was afraid she was ill. I couldn't say anything. I was just overwhelmed by a dark heavy anger, remembering how he had dismissed me when I had said the same thing to him years earlier.

Five years after I left home she took a massive overdose, believing my father was going out for the day; but he returned after just ten minutes because he had forgotten his wallet. He took her to the general hospital, where she was stomach-pumped and remained there for four days until she recovered physically. During the years I shouldered the burden of her overdoses and electric shock treatment, it was always, 'Don't tell your father.' Now I was no longer at home, this time it was, 'Don't tell Ann,' so my father did not contact me. However, I had had a premonition that something was wrong (the emotional cords between us were still strong) and decided to go up to visit unannounced, arriving just as my father returned from transferring my mother to the psychiatric hospital for electric shock treatment (again) and ongoing counselling.

I lay in her bed that night and was overwhelmed with a feeling of utter desolation. I sobbed my heart out as I empathised with how she must have felt the night before she took the overdose: the absolute depths of despair she must have been in, the isolation and loneliness, rejection and abandonment, with no one to love her or make her feel loved.

As far as I know she never took an overdose again although her favourite line when anything went wrong was, 'I'll end it all.' Ironically, when she was actually dying (aged seventy-two years) she didn't at all want it to end!

I left home when I was twenty, moving to London with the boy next door (yes, the very same, the one I had fallen out with as a child). However, the emotional cords between my mother and me were strongly in place, and I would often go back 'home', as I still thought of it, even though I had not been happy there. I would travel up on the train, full of excitement and hope, but return disappointed and depressed. Whatever I was searching for was never going to come from my parents. But 200 miles away, with no telephone, no cars, how was my mother to dump all her emotional overload on to me? *By letter.* In those early years away from home, I came to dread the envelope coming through the door. It would sometimes take me up to three days before I could bring myself to open and read the letter, and it would often send me into a deep depression, although I never connected the two until I had therapy some years later. Of course, I was under immense pressure to write back. If I didn't do it regularly, it would be another example of how little I cared for her, or how I failed as I was not like a proper daughter should be. However, when I did reply, I could only bring myself to write politely about every day matters. Hence my next piece of writing:

LETTER WRITING

> Writing so politely,
> Skimming the surface with upright meaningless
>   words,

Words that quiver and quail as they balance on the
   precipice edge
Of the unspoken depths of foaming frothy feeling,
Jumbling beneath the tranquil surface
In a milling frenzy of frustration
Striving for an outlet,

Bursting to be poured forth in torrents of emotional
   adjectives:
Pain and confusion
Anger and disillusion –

But, expressionless and straight-backed,
Those polite words stand to attention in attitudes of
   stiff prose,
Showing nothing, giving nothing

Empty masks
Saying nothing, meaning nothing –
All for nothing.

A few years on I wrote a poem to explain why I had written 'Letter Writing', although I am not sure why I called it 'Self-pity'. I was probably feeling very sorry for myself, and yet it seems I did have some pity for my mother too.

Self-pity

She was two hundred miles away
And still she could destroy.
Two hundred miles and a letter would come,
A bombshell of hatred spilling out.

And once again I would be fragmented,
Broken into small, jagged pieces
With the overwhelming urge to hit back,
To write down what I really felt,
Collect my feelings into one single point of attack
And show her finally just what she had done.

> But I was the only one left –
> Could I take away her prop?
> So I write words that cannot be seen through –
> Polite and restrained to the last full-stop!

My mother had a history of rejection and abandonment. She was abandoned at the age of two years by both her parents. Her father left her with his parents-in-law with the proviso that she was to be brought up a Catholic, and was never heard from again. Her mother went on to live with and eventually marry another man, with whom she had five more daughters, including twins, but hid from all of them that she had been married before or that she already had children. Then, at the age of ten, my mother was visiting 'Auntie May', who took her to one side and told her that *she* was her mother, and the person she thought was her mother was in fact her grandmother. However, it was a secret and she must not tell anyone else. A relative of her husband then called round and asked, 'Who's this little girl?' to which the reply was, 'Oh, that's just a neighbour's child – run along now.' My mother ran along.

The story goes that when my great-grandmother heard what had happened, she didn't say anything, just put on her coat, pinned on her hat (this was 1929) and marched off to have a few words with her daughter for this gross piece of selfishness, insensitivity and downright cruelty (my words). My poor mother... She then had to watch as her five half-sisters lived in a large house and garden, wore new clothes, went to good schools and had plenty of money, while she was the poor relation wearing hand-me-down clothes, with her grandfather walking miles to collect his dole money, on which they eked out a living.

UNDERSTANDING

> Yes, I am as you think of me –
> No capacity for feeling, no sensitivity –
> As independent as the water is clear.

> And you must never know
> Just how you battered me
> For that final burden is not deserved.
>
> Just as your own potential was unlimited
> Until those early years bruised and damaged,
> And you cried out in the midst of rejection
> And no one, no one, ever heard.

My mother doted on her grandfather and was devastated when he died in 1941 (on the same day as my father's mother died), and when during the following year she met my father at the factory they worked in, she and her grandmother needed a man to take care of them and he needed a home to live in and make his own. A Welshman, he had had to leave his home behind to seek work. My father was twelve years older than my mother, who appeared to be looking to replace her grandfather. They married, and a year later I came along. Forever more, she mourned her grandfather, and my father just could not compare. His was a different personality from the loving, warm, fun person he was supposed to replace.

In later years, when my mother and I were in telephone contact, there were not so many letters. I was expected to phone her and would often delay because I never knew what sort of response I would have. It could be, 'Oh, I'm glad you phoned, I wanted to tell you...' and I would sigh in relief. Or it could be the dismissive, 'Oh, it's you,' and my heart would sink, my mind cloud and my mood drop. It was the same with her birthday and Christmas cards. It was either, 'Lots of love, Mum' or the more ominous, 'From Mother' – depending on her mood. And woe betide I should ever forget to acknowledge Mother's Day. I remember planning to go up on one such Sunday as a surprise. Knowing her, I sent a card three or four days earlier so that she would not think I had forgotten. When I arrived she was shocked. She had just been telling a neighbour that she had heard nothing from me (the card had failed to arrive in time) and that it was the 'usual case of out of sight, out of mind'.

Looking back, you could say the good thing about her is that I always knew where she was coming from. Childlike, there was an honesty in her expression, even though she took no responsibility for any of her emotions. It was not hidden, as with my father or me. Because we hid and suppressed our emotions, neither of us could tolerate the powerful, raw intense emotion that came out of my mother. If there was a cowboy film on television and the horses were falling in battle, she would be wincing, catching her breath and moaning out loud at the thought they might be hurt. Similarly, there would be sighing with the love scenes, and if sex came into it, there would be tutting and straightening her clothes as her discomfort mounted. We knew always what she was feeling. It spilled out of her in waves.

Depression and suicide or attempted suicide seems to have been a theme in the female side of our family, because many years later I learned that her youngest half-sister, Wendy, 'drove off Beachy Head, leaving behind three children and a bastard husband', as one of her sisters told me. I had traced the twins from when their picture was published in one of the Sunday papers' magazines, and spoke to them once on the telephone. They still did not know my mother was their eldest half-sister. I didn't enlighten them. It was my mother's story not mine. She hadn't heard from any of them, including her real mother, since her twenties. Separately, she saw the picture too and sent it to me, but didn't want to pursue it. Too many years had gone by and there was too much emotion attached to the memories. Her real mother, May, had severed her connection with her own mother when I was about five. Apparently there was another falling-out. The last words May said to my mother were, 'She's really turned you against me, hasn't she?' It didn't seem to have occurred to her that maybe her own behaviour had contributed.

Becoming a Mother

In my late twenties, I had two beloved children, a girl and a boy, but couldn't find the right rhyme in the next poem, hence the 'two small boys'. Having children changed me. They were a large part of my growing up, although looking back I don't think I was very good at being a mother. I was too depressed, angry, damaged.

When in the grip of depression, there is an emotional withdrawal, a disconnection, so that there were many times I was not there for them in a warm and loving way. Depression highlights weaknesses. As one of my basic beliefs was that I was not good enough, this could easily translate to 'they would be better off without me'. On the other hand, there were other times when I was there, functioning as best I could and above all appreciating them.

THE LULL

Tea is over, bath time past,
They're both in bed at long last.

Silence reigns as we look around
At the chaos which is now to be found.
A battlefield of scattered toys,
Treasured possessions of two small boys.

The sink is full of dirty pots,
So many needed for such small tots.
Washing and ironing, the cleaning too,
Daytime jobs there's no time to do.

Suppertime, and a well-earned rest,
We've just come through another test.
The floors are tidy, the pots are clean,
The chaos that was is but a dream.

There's nothing to show that, come the next day,
Two sleeping angels will recommence play!

I had a moment of awareness when my daughter was about six years old and I noticed her long hair had not been brushed. Life was hectic by then, much changed from a decade earlier. We were doing many things – running our own much larger business and following my husband round while he raced motor cars, followed by dinghy racing and then yacht sailing. We were also socialising a lot, and the only way I could cope with this was by drinking heavily – at parties, dinner parties (the sort with three different desserts that all had to be home-made!), theatres, pubs, outings, all with a large group of friends. Often we had the children with us upstairs in sleeping bags while we partied and drank. I was also sorting out the children, ferrying them to school and to all their activities. I was out many evenings, as I belonged to various groups and also babysat other children in return for their mums doing the same for me. I was also studying (as always), dealing with depression and hooked on tranquillisers: all activities designed to prevent looking inwards, to ignore what was going on inside.

Ragged Hair

Ragged flowers, ragged hair,
An atmosphere of ragged care;

The rooms untidy, thrown about,
Scant attention causes doubt;

Rushing out, always late,
No time to make that special date;

Clothes flung on, unmade-up face,
A race for time at frantic pace,

Running from the lack of warmth.

I would have given my eye teeth to prevent my children being hurt by the way we were bringing them up. Later, when I became more aware, I became weighed down with burdens of guilt and remorse at the damage we had inflicted. I brought up my children trying to give them a very different sort of life from mine, trying very hard not to use emotional blackmail and manipulation as my mother had, determined that if ever my marriage was not working, I would not continue in it as my parents had – living in separate rooms, fighting when they met, wrecking the house, using me as the go-between. Unfortunately, I was not aware enough to realise that my depression was producing the same emotional deprivation as my mother's had on me; nor that my divorce would raise trust and abandonment issues for them; nor that, as my daughter's blueprint for this lifetime was to experience emotional blackmail and manipulation, she would do so when she began her relationship with her stepmother. I had had the best of intentions, but still it was not 'good enough' for them.

After the years of guilt, I came to realise I had done the best I could, given the low level of awareness I had at the time. I am aware now that at the soul level my children chose me for the experience of family life that I provided for them, imperfect as it was at the personality level, as they were the very experiences they needed to fulfil their own spiritual missions. I have since acknowledged to them my deficiencies as a mother and, with their forgiveness (didn't I say they were beloved?), I have left behind the years of guilt that increasing awareness had brought on. Like all parents, if I had known better I would have done it differently.

More importantly I learned there was still something I could do to make up for it, and that was to effect my own healing. Healing ourselves is our greatest gift to our children (and our family), as it provides them with the example of how they too can achieve their own healing, their own release of karma, their own self-realisation and spiritual unfolding.

Relationship Breakdown

I never really had a relationship with my father. He was not comfortable around me, as I was a girl, and he communicated with me through my mother. His belief was that girls should be brought up by women. Added to this, I was completely brainwashed as to how awful he was, to the extent that in my late teens I ended up hating him. The only emotion I ever picked up from him was disapproval. I was very wary of him and I didn't know why until many years later. It was not really until I left home and my mother's influence slowly waned that I began to feel sorry for him.

From empathising and trying to make it better for my mother, away from her influence I started to feel anger and resentment. At the same time, I was wracked with guilt because I believed it was bad to hate your parents when you were supposed to love them. One of my mother's many sayings was 'I'm your mother, you should love me.' The very first therapy workshop I ever attended (now in my thirties) was on guilt. I went there because my father had had his first stroke and I felt very guilty because I did not want to go and visit my parents. This felt so wrong because I 'ought' to want to. I did go because I was still very much guided by all these 'shoulds' and 'oughts' I had learned from them. I was their only daughter, their only child, how could I not be there for them?

After the advice given to me at the guilt workshop, I embarked on weekly therapy sessions where I learned about manipulation and emotional blackmail. My mother's greatest manipulation was 'If you loved me, you would…' Then she would tell me what she wanted me to do, like the time in my early teens when she wanted me to go to my father and ask him to make up with her, but I was not to say it was her idea. They had not been talking for a few days. (If we sat down to a meal, just the three of us, it would be 'Ann, ask your father to pass the salt', and so on.) I cringed at the thought but I did it because I couldn't say no to her. That would mean I didn't love her and it would prove what a bad person I was. I suffered agonies doing it; the feelings were so indescribable I just wanted to go somewhere and hide. As I was leaving the room (escaping), I blurted out, 'Mum didn't tell me to ask you.' He knew, it was so obvious – I was no good at this sort of thing.

During the eighteen months of therapy I came to realise that some of my depressions didn't just come out of nowhere. They could be triggered, such as when I received a letter from my mother. Up to then I had not understood that some of the depressions could have a reason, that they could be a reaction to something. I learned how influenced I was by other people's needs and that I yearned for approval. I had no awareness of my own needs and sank (became depressed) in the face of disapproval.

One memory has just surfaced about those letters. I took one in for my therapist to read and she said, 'She's writing to her mother.' That made a lot of sense. Also, it lifted some of the burden of guilt from my shoulders. Maybe it wasn't all my fault after all!

I remember vividly though that there was one thing I could not reveal to my therapist, because I felt such shame about it. The one thing she must never find out was that inside of me was just a black hole. There was nothing there. I had to keep anyone else from knowing this, otherwise I would be found out just how unworthy a person I really was. I had to keep playing this part in the world outside so that people would not guess how unlike everyone else I was. I was fairly intelligent and yet I was so emotionally damaged I believed this to be real!

I mentioned earlier that we were socialising hard, and sometimes it was impossible, no matter how much I drank, to cover up the depression, the pretence that I belonged.

THE PARTY

In desperation, I look around...

Surrounded by people, playing their roles,
I stand in the centre, a smiling mask,
Listening to words and shrilling laughter,
I hear only noise and emptiness.
An onlooker with the cracks well hidden.

I cry out silently –
Just one look of awareness
To pierce the walls of isolation,
Just one look of understanding
To melt the ice of loneliness.

In desperation, I look around...

As the decade progressed, I was becoming more unstable. I was taking tranquillisers but the depression was becoming much worse. On one occasion I swallowed a lot of tranquillisers, more in hysteria than anything else; after all, my husband was in the house at the time. After a night in hospital I became a psychiatric outpatient for a while and I was put on a strong dose of anti-depressants. These initially resulted in nightmares during which, terrified, I would literally jump out of bed, screaming, to huddle in a corner cowering.

So, having a cold, distant relationship with my father did not really prepare me for a long-lasting happy relationship with my first husband. In the late 1970s, my marriage was breaking down. My then husband had the same numerological numbers as my father (go figure!), and similarly could not express feelings or emotions. At times, I was really struggling with the depression and filled with a lot of bitterness (probably much of it was from childhood, but I didn't know this then). This bitterness overflowed one time when, on a visit to my childhood home, I was lying in bed unable to sleep, so I wrote the following. It appears to be very anti-men – the cause of all our problems, according to my mother!

Man-made

Lying awake –
Street light, electric
Patterns the ceiling
Bathes the sleeping children:
Man-made light.

Listen –
Instant droning television
Revving car growling by
Distant trains rushing on:
Man-made toys.

Noise, not sounds
Dark walls, not clear sky
Steel speed, not wandering clouds:
Man-made steel.

> Surrounded, I am part of this
> Made in Manchester, by man for man.
>
> Isolated, I hide behind the walls
> Of a fleshy, puppet body-mask:
> Man-made mask.
>
> I look out
> But no one sees me watching.

We separated. I was thirty-five years old and a single mother with two children aged nine and seven and a half. I went to university to study for a law degree, graduating three years later with first class honours much to my total surprise! So much so, that I remember crying because my father would never know – he had died two years previously. I still wanted to gain his approval! I had refused to apply for university when I was at school and my father was very disappointed in me (as my mother relayed to me). The reason I refused was that we were told that an important part of university was the social side as well as the studying. Hearing this, I was so filled with dread that I had nightmares. Back then I just didn't have a social life. I was shy, self-conscious, had a chronic lack of confidence and was so busy hiding all my 'secrets' about my home life, the black hole inside of me and the depressions that I couldn't relax. I didn't know how to enjoy myself back then. I didn't know how to relax with people. I didn't know how to *be*.

My father had died a year into my degree. By this time he had had three strokes and went into hospital to have a gangrenous leg amputated. I visited him the day after the operation. He was sitting up in bed, extremely weak, and there was a nurse standing partially in front of me. I noticed he was trying to lean forward to see me. I moved to look at him and for that brief moment his eyes were shining, filled with love. It was the first and only time that he showed me he did in fact love me, although he was unaware of what he was doing and did not even remember afterwards that I had been there. I was numb with surprise.

He died some weeks later but I had not seen him again. My

focus as usual was on my mother and how she was coping. I was due to go up when my mother called to say he had gone. She said he had been asking where I was. If only she had told me earlier… If I thought he wanted to see me, I would have gone like a shot. For a long time I blamed her for withholding that information, believing that as usual she had come between us. I felt such remorse about not seeing him again before he died that when my mother was in a hospice years later, I insisted both my children visit her while she was alive, so that she would know she was cared for.

During the period after my separation and eventual divorce, I also moved house, worked part time in advice and social care centres, had a part-time cleaning job, drank with friends, had affairs and, after the degree, went back into full-time employment. Although at the time my relationship breakdown produced a lot of strong negative emotions, including a lot of anger, these long years later I can see that it was in fact a very positive experience, as it changed my life completely and shook me very forcefully out of one way of being and plunged me into another. What it was doing to the children is another story, but that is their journey.

I was also a volunteer at the Samaritans. I learned a lot about suicide and attempted suicide, whether it was a cry for help or a real intention to end a life. Often people just wanted respite, oblivion until all the darkness had dissipated, all the problems and worries were over. I met some wonderful people working there, one man in particular called Paul. He had such great inner wisdom and almost a guardian angel quality. It was a privilege to share a duty with him. Talking to him about my parents he once asked me why I was going to visit. Was it out of love or out of conscience? At the time, I replied, 'Conscience.'

There were all types and all ages of people volunteering. What they had in common was the ability to listen without judgment. One of the most important things they taught me was to trust my feelings. 'What did you feel about it?' 'Does it ring true?' 'Is this all there is or is there something deeper?' I have sometimes wondered if my stint at the Samaritans was a way of exorcising all my mother's suicide attempts – to face the fact of suicide head-on, so that it lost the power I had attached to it because of my history. The word used to fill me with dread before then. Another reason I was a volunteer was because there was a part of me that wished to be of service, to help others.

Like many women of my generation, I embraced feminism, and during this time I began taking part in women's 'consciousness-raising' groups. I also became a member of a feminist organisation whose aim was to lobby for changes in the law in order to give women more equality. I remember the anger I felt when my children were born and for the first four years of their lives, before the law was changed, I was not held to be fit enough to be their legal guardian, merely because I was a woman. Only the father could be that. Yet I was the one who was bringing them up, making all the decisions for them, had had the better education, and so on. I was also rebelling against the rigid roles and views of my parents. My mother's favourite expression to my father was, 'You're the man, you're supposed to know.' She wasn't joking, she meant it – she believed it!

On my divorce, I changed my name back to my birth name. My father had two sisters, each of whom had sons. He was the only one with a girl, so the name would die out. It seemed important for me to continue the family name for as long as possible. Now I realise I was changing back to the energies contained in the numbers. In numerology, our date of birth and our names provide us with information as to who we are and what we are here to learn. Those energies influence us, guide us. I felt I had come in with this name for a reason. It represented my potential, the one I was striving to reach in this lifetime. It contains a clarity that speaks to me. The name is me. I have not changed it since, even when I remarried.

After five years without a partner, I began to live with my second husband-to-be. This provided me with another quite different relationship experience from which to grow and develop even more. Through many trials and tribulations, we have moved, for the most part, into calm, harmonious waters.

2. The Middle Years

BECOMING AWARE

As a result of the Harmonic Convergence* in 1987, like many others I started to awaken spiritually, very slowly at first. One evening, I found myself in a stress and self-awareness class, with the teacher saying that she believed in life after death. I remember having such a strong reaction, thinking, *What on earth am I doing here?* For I believed this life was all there was. This was the product of a Catholic mother, an atheist father and a Protestant Sunday school, followed by the rejection of religion in my late teens. Yet for three years I continued with this evening class learning about 'weird and wonderful' stuff like chakras and the importance of colour, the wisdom of dolphins, psychometry, intuition, meditation, healing, the soul, reincarnation, astrology, numerology... Oh, the excitement, the studying and learning, the experiences, the insights! I was soaking it all up like water in a parched land. I began to experience the resonance of truth – a heartfelt jolt of recognition when I heard something that I knew to be true – my first conscious experience of inner knowing. I realised that the world was not as concrete as it seemed, that there was a whole new dimension I had previously failed to see.

Without really realising what I was doing, I was embarking on a journey of self-discovery. Who was I? What were my strengths and weaknesses? What was hiding beneath the anger and depression? If I could lay all that to rest, who could I become? I began to gain some understanding of who I was. I came to realise I had a body, a mind, feelings and emotions, all of which formed my personality, and so I started to explore these different parts of me.

---

* Harmonic Convergence: an unusual formation of planets which heralded a new spiritual awakening on Earth.

The Body

We all learn at a very young age that it is more comfortable for us if we can distance ourselves from emotional and physical discomfort. We feel so overwhelmed by this discomfort that we learn coping mechanisms, such as working all hours or exercising till we drop, so that we never have to stop and confront what is happening inside of us. Or we might feel so overwhelmed with raw emotional, and subsequent physical, discomfort that we turn to outside help to try to suppress these feelings, such as painkillers, tranquillisers, antidepressants, alcohol or drugs. My mother spent years on painkillers and antidepressants of one kind or another, and even in her last years still sat down at four o'clock each day for a cup of tea and a codeine. Of course, her electric shock treatment was the ultimate suppressor for her.

We can cultivate the ability to believe we are feeling something totally different. Instead of feeling afraid or hurt, I would believe I was just angry or depressed. I couldn't feel the fear or hurt because I was so used to masking such vulnerability with the anger which would then transmute into depression. Some would not feel anything at all. This process of denial can arise over a period of time or it can be a one-off incident of extreme effectiveness. A friend of mine told me that when she was four years old she was in a strange bed, crying, because she was desperately afraid of the dark and no light had been left on for her. After a long time, an aunt came up and immediately started beating her for not going to sleep – no questions as to why, no compassion as to how. In that instant, my friend learned she was not allowed to express her fears; in fact, she was not allowed to express herself at all. Better then not to feel them in the first place.

I learned that one of my ways of coping was to stay purely in my mind, forever thinking and analysing and rationalising, because while I thought, I couldn't feel; and thus I cut myself off from anything emotional or physical that might be unsettling. For a large part of my life, I was so out of touch with my body that I was able to go to the dentist for years and not need an injection when I had a tooth filled! I had cut myself off from the natural pain my body was feeling. Another example was when my young husband was involved in a multiple pile-up at the start of a motor race. I had watched his car turn end over end, and he was trapped underneath. When a while later I was allowed into the medical tent I went to him and the ambulance men started saying something to me. However, I was almost immediately hustled away out of his sight and made to sit down by the nurse while she treated me for shock. I was puzzled because I had not felt there was anything wrong with me. I do remember not really taking in why the ambulance couldn't leave yet. It wasn't until we were in the ambulance that I realised we had a police escort of two motorcycle riders (that's what the wait had been for), and they were going on ahead to hold up traffic at lights so that the ambulance would not have to stop and start. In fact, it travelled very slowly. They were worried that any jerking or jolting might damage my husband's spine further, but it still didn't penetrate to feeling level. It was as though it was all happening at a great distance from me.

Even today, now I am in touch with my body and feelings, if I receive a shock I find myself in that instant distancing myself from the pain (physical or emotional) and jumping into my mind. It enables me to cope until the 'emergency' is over.

So, I started to look at my body. I needed to become aware of it, to get back in touch with it.

My Body

> These hands of mine look tired,
> The skin wrinkled, the veins prominent.
> My hands, for all these years
> Doing always as I ask, never letting me down,
> These hands of mine are wearying.
>
> This body of mine is tired,
> Used and abused, scant looking after,
> More effort required to move and groove,
> More time spent just to keep it going,
> This body of mine is ageing.

Over these next years I began to shed the addictive habits I had needed to cope. I gave up smoking, followed a year later by dieting to lose the weight I had put on as a result of giving up smoking. I began to look at my eating habits and to bring in more healthy foods and drink more water. I reduced the socialising which meant I was cutting down on the alcohol, finally reaching the point where today my body cannot tolerate it. For thirteen years I had been dependent on antidepressants and tranquillisers, and I weaned myself off these over a few months. If I didn't take them, I couldn't sleep and became tense so it meant a few sleepless and strung-out months as I slowly reduced them! The final habit-forming substance I had to wean myself off was coffee.

DEAR BODY...

>This is my letter of apology; I have ignored you for too long,
>I feel the aches and pains but don't know what they mean.
>To give you what you need I need to learn your language.
>Tell me, how do I interpret your message?
>
>Listen to the wind in the trees,
>Listen to the water in the stream,
>Listen to the rustle in the undergrowth,
>Nature's sounds.
>
>Listen to the blood in my veins,
>Listen to the pumping of my heart,
>Listen to the breath in my lungs,
>I am also part of Nature.
>
>Listen to the pulsing, to the throb,
>To the rhythm of life coursing through me
>In tune with the Life Force all around.
>Listen to how I am feeling
>And then you will hear the message I bring.

I was slowly getting back in touch with my body, cleansing it, helping it to function more healthily, understanding it better. All this happened over quite a few years. I don't remember making a conscious decision to take myself in hand and improve my health. It seemed to happen organically – when the time was right, a new idea would pop into my mind. It was not until later that I came to realise more fully what I was doing and had been doing – bringing my body (and myself) *back into balance*. It was not until I was more balanced that I could begin to understand that I had begun the process of waking up.

DEAR BODY...

I undertake to give you constant awareness.
When you speak to me of something, I will give my immediate attention.

I will stop what is causing you distress, and change what needs to be changed.
I will fill your lungs deeply so that your blood sings full of oxygen and life force.
I will exercise to energise you, eat nutritious foods to nourish you and drink life-giving water to hydrate you.
I will endeavour to keep you properly rested, relaxed and balanced.

You are a treasured vehicle, whose job has been well done,
I will honour the experiences you bring me, the feelings you engender in me,
I will fully appreciate the joy of each sensation and the life force that flows through me.
I undertake to honour your wisdom and cherish you as you continue to carry me through life.

One thing I have found really helps me is to remember to breathe deeply. Often I am breathing quite shallowly without realising it. To pause and take in a long, slow, deep breath de-stresses the physical body, calms the emotions, and while you are focusing on the breath, your mind is still. You have brought yourself back to centre. A centenarian was being interviewed on the radio and was asked for his secret to a long life. He said, 'Eat porridge for breakfast and remember to keep breathing!' Well, I'm eating the porridge. I must also remember the breathing.

The Mind

Having the same propensity for an out of control mind as my mother had with her manic depression (she would often be up all night sewing, reading, cleaning or fretting), I came to realise that in some way I needed to learn how to bring my mind under some sort of control, to keep it clear and positive rather than allow it to run wild in obsessively agitated, negative thoughts, worries and even paranoia. The following is an example of my intuitive writing, that is writing a question and then just allowing the words to flow out. Looking at it now (years later), the writing seems confused, perhaps reflecting the confusion I was feeling around this time. How do I control my mind? The theory was far easier than the actual practice.

HOW DO I SWITCH OFF MY MIND?

How to switch off my mind?
Channel it
Down into the stillness of me,
Down through the raging inferno
To the calmness of me.

How to channel my mind?
Focus it, aim it, take it there.
To focus is to decide where to go,
To aim is to form the intention to go there
And then you go there, travel there.

Then stay with it,
Be with it,
Love it.

Eventually meditation and visualisation helped me as they enabled me to practise focusing my mind, for increasingly longer periods. In this way I learned how to still the mind so that just for the second, the minute, I was fully present. I understand that is the aim of meditation – finding our way to being in the moment, in the here and now. We need to learn to live in the present rather than thinking about the future or rehashing the past.

I learned that I had a powerful mind, which was very good at analysing, organising and understanding. I also learned that I was not my mind; it was part of me but not the whole of me. It was not in control, I was. I learned that my mind could not work out my own process, nor plan my next step, I needed to leave that to my higher mind, my soul, so I needed to keep my mind occupied by giving it projects to work on. To this day, I do lots of crosswords, read books, make lists, write, research projects, all just to keep my mind occupied while the real work of planning my next step is being done by my soul. This way is not for everyone; this is just for my type and how it works for me. An example of this is when I started to give up all my addictive props of smoking, overeating, alcohol and antidepressants. It had not been a conscious decision to clean up my act; rather it had been a decision made at the soul level, although at the time I was not aware enough to realise this.

The Emotions

At one point during this period I seemed to be replaying my childhood experience, where one part of my family would sit in one room and the other in another room. Which one should I sit in? I felt divided in two again. I felt impotent, powerless. I had no idea how to resolve the situation – just as I must have felt as a child.

Also at this same time a lot of anger was coming up. Most of it was unexpressed. However, at times it would spurt out of me when I least expected it, and onto people who did not deserve it (even though I thought they did at the time!). The expression of this anger was more in terms of irritation and impatience, snapping at others or 'telling them off' for some supposed transgression. I had some unhappy years at work where I seemed to be alienated from everyone, not helped by one of the women carrying out a whispering campaign against me. I was certainly manifesting my belief that I could not trust anyone. There came a point when I could not sleep at night and would sit up, filled with anger, my mind in overdrive with dark thoughts.

I don't remember what it was that triggered it but I have a memory of feeling such rage inside that I didn't know what to do with myself. So, early one evening after work I went to sit in a field, hoping to find some peace in nature. When I entered the field there were about ten horses clustered together in the field. I crossed over to the other side away from them and sat on a log but I couldn't calm the rage. It flooded me; I was lost in it. After a while I looked up and realised the horses were much nearer. They were coming towards me, looking at me. The ones at the front were almost prancing, turning one way and then the other, all the while coming nearer. It dawned on me that they were agitated because they were picking up on my rage. I felt nervous and started deep breathing, focusing on calming down, bringing myself back under control. I succeeded because eventually they stopped prancing and went back to grazing. They were quite close by now. I had no idea how powerful emotions are, how much energy we send out into the world and the distance it travels.

In 1995, still working full-time, I started a two-year part-time counsellor training course which turned into an unforeseen and unimaginable journey of self-discovery and awakening. At one point my own process became more important than becoming a counsellor, although I did eventually work through it all to qualify. It was a very spiritual group (about twenty of us), which suited me. It was also experiential, which meant that we learned from doing it ourselves rather than just theoretically.

I learned that my depression was not the deepest part of me, although it felt like it. Going down into that place inside of me felt as though there was no further down I could go, so dark and desperate a place was it, a prison from which there was no escape. Yet what the depression was doing was masking all the other feelings I could not cope with when I was young, feelings such as hurt and fear – all the vulnerable parts of me – and all these feelings lay under the depression. I discovered that below my depression lay fear, below the fear lay terror, and that this terrified part of me was my hurt and wounded inner child.

It was during one of our group sessions that one of the men shouted, and there was a tone in the voice (male domination and violence) that triggered something in me. I felt as though I was breaking up or shattering inside. All I could see were swirling, formless atoms. I was looking on chaos and falling apart into it. Then the word 'childhood' slowly crossed the screen of my third eye. This word told me that what I was experiencing was from childhood and was not the reality of now. I was brought out of it by the person next to me asking if I was all right. Apparently I had gone ashen. The fundamental fear of all souls is annihilation of the self. In other words, we are afraid that innermost life spark will be destroyed. When this part of us feels threatened in any way, it takes avoiding action. This was what the very core of me, my inner child, had experienced. To prevent that perceived fragmentation, it had sought to protect itself by locking itself away where it could not be harmed.

THE LOST CHILD

I was born, fully alive, open and trusting –
No protection, no armour.

And then I found that I was not the centre of the Universe
Because if I was, all my needs would be met, and they weren't.

And I was surrounded by coldness, by loud, frightening noises,
By black, swirling anger and darkness,
And I reached out for comfort, but none was given, no one was there.

Annihilation lay before me; I was falling into chaos,
   fragmenting into pieces.
Terrified, I fought to save myself, and locked myself
   away where I could not be harmed
In an infinite space of blackness, suspended, frozen,
   waiting.

And she forgot that I existed:
No matter how much I shouted and sobbed, she did
   not hear me,
No matter how I pleaded and whispered, she was not
   listening.

And I was left behind with fear to protect me,
So that when life was in danger of getting too close to me
She became afraid and ran away.

But she was only half alive
Not knowing why she had this dark emptiness inside her
Not knowing what it was that she was protecting
Not knowing who it was that she had forgotten...

And I waited, suspended, frozen
In that infinite space of blackness.

I had a very real need to understand what was happening. According to numerology, it is part of my life path, which is to learn the peace of mind that comes with knowing myself; to analyse and seek to understand myself, others and the world about me; and to develop until I reach the highest levels of wisdom. 'The Lost Child' above was written to express the experience of what had happened. My need to analyse it in order to understand what had happened then led me to write the following.

LOOKING BACK

The very first time I experienced terror,
To preserve my Self I 'ran away'.
And so it was all my life, fear and flight,
Get angry, walk away or collapse deep inside –
Withdrawing from the world, hiding away where no
   one could see.

The fear was of the anger spilling out of control
Because to be out of control might mean the terror
   could be released
And that was unthinkable.

What was this terror? What happened all that time ago?

Annihilation of the Self results in fragmentation into
   chaos
And suddenly there I was, falling apart inside –
I was looking on chaos, swirling formless atoms
Seeing and feeling chaos, annihilation loomed.

Terrified I took evasive action to save my Self and
   locked her away,
My inner child, my core, my creativity, my essence,
Froze her in time, suspended in a space of infinite
   blackness.

And to protect her, another self remained behind –
   my Fear Self
Who would trigger the flight mechanism
Should anything threaten to get too near to her.

But these feelings of fear and terror were too raw and
   intense
Ever to be felt again,
So I masked them with anger and depression,
More familiar and so more comfortable.

> The rest of me grew up surviving with the help of my defences,
> But I was not whole; I had left behind the core of me:
> My inner child, frozen in time, had been forgotten.

However, I still hadn't touched on what had triggered off this terror or when this had occurred. It couldn't be hearing my father when I was eleven, because we lose the inner child much earlier, any time between birth to seven years or so.

What is the inner child? It's that part of us that is our essence, the very core of us, and it can become damaged, so that we build layers on top of it to keep it safe or to distance ourselves from the hurt. Another way of explaining it would be to say that when we are born our heart centre is wide open. However, needing to protect ourselves, we close it off. Or we could say our consciousness or awareness was arrested or frozen at a very young age.

Your traumatised inner child waits until it feels safe to be present. If you have reached a point in your life when you are feeling stuck with no seeming way forward, it may be that the time has come to reach back to collect and integrate those parts of you that were frozen or split off in your early years. Alternatively, it will happen organically with no seeming conscious decision on your part – almost in spite of yourself! However it happens, once whole again, you move forward.

RECOVERING THE INNER CHILD

Some months after the 'looking on chaos' experience, we had a two-day encounter weekend, which is where the group would sit together and wait for whatever came up. It would replay how we were in our primary groups, so that a lot of childhood issues and feelings would arise. I had been extremely anxious about doing this, worried at possible confrontation and being told by everyone what they really thought of me, because, of course, it could not be good.

However, I had learned by now that I needed to go through these experiences, despite my almost overwhelming fear, because this was the only way for me to really change at a very deep level.

It was part of my growth process. If I could face all my deepest feelings – to meet and experience each one in turn – then I would be freed from their hold on me. Often fear holds us back from looking at these feelings. After all, we've spent a lifetime trying not to re-experience them. After starting this course it was not long before I felt that I had been backed into a corner, that there was nowhere else to hide from all the stuff that was now bubbling up inside me. The only option left was to turn and face it all.

The first day of the encounter weekend was stressful, with only one verbal attack on me, which I somehow fielded. The next day, after only three hours' sleep (I was so wound up) I broke down at lunchtime, sobbing that I couldn't go on. I had hidden away in a small room and was sitting in the corner my head down in my hands. A friend found me and comforted me, offering me a large red apple to eat, which nourished me immediately. My blood sugar level must have been very low. When I calmed down she told me to look up, and there were also three other friends standing, watching over me like Guardian Angels. It was a profound moment, a beautiful, heart-warming moment, because it felt as though they were Guardian Angels who were there to hold me up while I was feeling weak, giving me the strength and encouragement to go on.

After lunch they brought out a large mattress and baseball bats, as some of the group wanted to express their anger. They started banging and shouting. Acting purely on instinct (as normally I wouldn't draw attention to myself), I ran to hide behind the seats saying, 'I can't cope with this!' After a while I saw the door – an escape route – and ran out, closing it behind me.

Only then did I just 'hear' the noise of the anger and violence, and then I knew what I was escaping from. It was the *sound* that I was running from. It had triggered off how I had felt when for the first time I heard the violent energy of my father shouting and banging downstairs. Too young to have visual memories, I had remembered at a cellular level. Because I was too young to physically run anywhere, I had to run away inside of myself, so my safe place then was locking myself away in a void and blotting it all out. I was now re-enacting what I had metaphorically done at the age of a few weeks, and I needed to escape to a place where I could not hear the sound. I ended up in the reception room two floors down. I was sobbing my heart out.

At the same time, there arose inside of me an awareness which knew that I was finally crying for that part of me that had been locked away and which I had now got in touch with – my terrified self, my inner child. She was there at long last, and I could finally cry for her and for her suffering and hurt and pain and terror. I was now in touch with it all. The black hole inside of me was no more. All the trapped feelings and emotions were there. My aware self allowed me to realise what was happening, and when someone came to sit with me I was able to say, amid the sobs, 'It's OK, I know what's happening.'

I didn't want to go back to the group, and thought I could walk away, saying, 'I don't want to be part of this' (something I could not do as a child). However, the facilitator was infinitely wiser than I was about what was happening and eventually came down to say I had to go back. If there ever came a time when I was counselling someone who reached the same depth and ran away from it, they needed to know on an unconscious level that they could trust me enough to know they could come back, because when it had happened to me I had also 'gone back'. I did go back, hugging a cushion (representing my inner child) to me, although I experienced a lot of fear at the thought of the group looking at me as I went back in. She walked in front of me so that I could hide behind her!

I know now that I had indeed heard my father much earlier than I remembered consciously; in fact, when I was only a few weeks old. I learned that the first time I heard this violent shouting I had been terrified but no one had come. The shock of it had so traumatised me that my inner child, the very core or essence of me, fearing it was under threat and would be destroyed, had hidden away to protect itself.

FINDING MY INNER CHILD

> There came a time when the depression no longer did its job
> The defences were weakening, the anger was taking over.

> And then the strong and overwhelming feeling
> That I was backed into a corner
> And the only thing left for me was to turn and face the fear,
> Because it was fear that had brought me to this corner,
> A fear I had carried with me all my life
> But had never recognised it before.
>
> And then one last time I ran away,
> But this time I remembered the terror, felt it again
> And sobbing my heart out, I learned how to take care of me
> Because my aware self knew that I was finally crying
> For the part of me that had been locked away
> Since those very early days
> And which I had now got in touch with –
> My terrified self, my inner child –
> She was finally there and I could at last cry for her,
> For her suffering and hurt and pain and terror.

A few days later, when someone took up the bat again, I stayed in the room. I was sitting on the floor, legs stretched out before me. Each time he shouted and hit, my whole body lifted off the floor – I had a sense of a baby in a pram which, when shocked, feels it all over and its body quite literally 'jumps'. So the age when I locked myself away out of harm's way was very early, as a baby in a cot, listening to the violent sounds, being terrified by the dark, raw energy and no one coming to reassure me. The next day my solar plexus felt red raw. If I breathed in deeply or laughed, it would hurt.

I stopped going to the group and would come home from work exhausted, and all I could do was lie down on the bed and nurse myself until I felt better – to care for my inner child for the first time, as no one had been there to care for her all those years ago. I was 'manic' for nine weeks. I replayed the incidents over and over again in my mind. I started to have only three hours' sleep at night. I was ungrounded and out of balance. It had knocked me for six. I was locked in my head because I could not bear to feel – it was literally too raw.

QUESTIONS TO MY INNER CHILD

Where were you?
I was here all along.

Why didn't I know you were missing?
You never looked inwards.

Why didn't I hear you?
You weren't listening in my direction.

Why didn't I feel you?
You were too distant to make the connection.

What were you doing?
I was waiting for you to come.

What do I do now?
Take me with you, wherever you go.

Here is my hand – I won't let go.

After getting in touch with the deepest part of me and the terror that I had suppressed all my life, there then began a period of healing. It took a while to recover. All my feelings and emotions were exposed and I felt very fragile. I needed to re-experience all those emotions that I had felt as a child but had successfully buried under anger and depression. The fear of these emotions had held me in a grip of paralysis all my life, doing everything I could to protect myself against ever feeling them again. It was only in the reliving of these terrifying feelings and emotions, and the learning that I would not be destroyed by them, that I could start the process of becoming fully alive. I was physically shaking when I went back into the group. I felt total alienation from everyone and a rising hatred of the authority figures (the facilitators), who represented my parents.

The more I began to get in touch with my feelings the more I also understood about defence patterns – how we had certain ways in which to protect ourselves from other people and the world outside us. My pattern was collapsing down inside myself and disconnecting (hiding), so that no one could get to me. This was what my mother had not been able to cope with: my apparent lack of reaction, the seeming indifference. Unconsciously, she could feel the withdrawal, the separation. In fact, I discovered my collapse inwards took me to the same place that my depressions took me. My mother's pattern was controlling either by overpowering me (the tirades) or by undermining me (the manipulation and emotional blackmail). Mentally learning and understanding about these defence or protective patterns was only part of the process. To truly understand, I had to experience them.

So it was shortly after this that I have a memory of an incident at work. I was working for a woman who was really lovely, a good person, a practising Christian. We could talk for hours, really connecting at a deep level. However, her defence pattern was to undermine. A perfectionist, she would continually criticise (very nicely), and she would make little laughing comments that were like barbs. When anyone reacted, she would say, 'I was only joking.' She was very interested in you and found out a great deal about you, which she could later use (very subtly) against you. Within six months I felt so broken down I started crying at work and I couldn't quite put my finger on what was happening. Her being so friendly and such a seemingly genuinely lovely person confused me. As my course continued, I realised what she was doing. My relationship with her taught me so much about how I react to this type of controlling behaviour. (She was brought up with dominant, successful parents and brothers, so this had been her way of not getting squashed in childhood. However, she was unaware of what she was doing and could never understand why people did not want to work for her or with her, or were very wary of her.)

On one occasion, we had just had a wonderfully friendly

conversation and she turned away saying, laughingly, 'I must go to try and get in touch with a counsellor for this case – a proper one, not one who's trained part-time.'

As I was doing my training part time, it was obvious at whom this barbed comment was thrown. It came out of the blue. It felt like a knife being stabbed into me. Yet, for the first time in my life, instead of reacting in anger or my famous collapsing into depression, I sat there feeling bewildered, stunned almost. Where had that come from? Why had it come? Didn't she believe what I was doing was 'proper'? Why had she seemed so supportive if she didn't? After the bewilderment I felt hurt. Then I thought, *Wow, I'm feeling, just feeling – purely and simply. I haven't masked the hurt with anger. I haven't withdrawn. I haven't descended into depression. I'm still here.*

This realisation was like a light going on. As well as feeling hurt and slightly shocked, at another level I was also feeling *Wow!* That's all my inner child had needed – for me to listen to what she was really feeling, and for me to accept that it was OK for her to feel this way. No longer did she need to hide these feelings.

I was now very aware of my spirituality, yet this boss would often shake her head and say, 'If only you could have faith.' She could not understand a spirituality outside of a religion. I'm not saying that spirituality is *only* to be found outside religion. For me it was, but there are many beautiful, very spiritual beings who have found that aspect of themselves within religion. There are many roads but in the end they all lead to the same place.

The more I got in touch with and accepted all my feelings the less I became depressed. If I did have a reaction and retreated into that depressed/collapsed space, the sooner I came out of it. I was taking back control. Instead of being an emotional victim overwhelmed by whatever emotion was raging throughout my body, I was learning to be aware of each feeling, accepting it, releasing it and moving on. All this took place over quite a few years.

It was also a question of finding out what my inner child's needs (that is, my needs) were and finding out how to get them met. Assertiveness training tells you how to assert your needs, but what if you don't know what they are in the first place? If you've been overwhelmed all your life by the feelings and needs of others, there's never been any space in which to find out what is right for you. Being empathic has been brilliant for listening to people, understanding them, soothing them and helping them heal, but it has been a curse where my own needs are concerned. I needed to learn how to detach, to disentangle myself from other people's feelings and emotions, to realise they were not mine. I had a lot of learning still to do.

EMPOWERMENT

The counsellor training course was drawing to a close, finishing with a further encounter group, this time a five-day intensive. In the final few weeks I had become a part of the group, feeling comfortable enough and trusting it enough to speak out and express myself. From remaining huddled and shivering on the riverbank, I had now jumped into the water and was swimming comfortably but it had taken almost two years to reach that point.

I could not do this at the beginning – I was still hiding by staying outside of the group, just as I had in my primary family group when it had been safer not to draw attention to myself and to wait to see what sort of mood was afoot before bringing the attention to me. To speak out in the group was not on, because it drew attention to me. I remember one time when the guy next to me started telling the group about how well I had just counselled someone. I was squirming with embarrassment and silently wishing he would shut up. The embarrassment was not because he was saying nice things about me; it was because in doing so he was drawing everyone's attention to me. To cap it all, the facilitator then asked me a question, and when I answered it briefly I looked around at the group and it seemed as if they had all turned into grey stone statues, frozen in eternity, their eyes turned blankly on me. It was as if no one there was hearing or comprehending me. There was no warmth or understanding coming my way – no humanity. Perhaps this is how I had felt as a child. I felt small and timid and excruciatingly shy, like I imagine a little mouse trapped in the gaze of a cat. (My nickname at school had been 'mousy' – short for field mouse.) Perhaps also the grey stone statues were a projection of the way I would freeze inside when I was younger.

Another strong reaction I had in the group was when part of the group turned on a guy I was sitting next to (the same one as above). We were facing them, and suddenly it seemed as if there was all this cold, frightening, dark energy coming at me, and I broke down. It was actually being focused on him. If it had been me, I have doubts if I could have continued the course. What it had triggered was the root cause of my hating to be the centre of attention. It was karmic, and came from a past life memory in which I was burnt as a witch. It was not the actual burning but the moment before when I was surrounded by a howling, baying mob. All that powerful negative energy of hate and anger pouring over me was overwhelming; it felt like my very soul was being destroyed. In a past life regression this is what I re-experienced, and it jolted me so much I didn't want to do any others. Later, at an intuitive writing weekend, we tuned into a past life experience and this one came up again. The words flowed out of me. Next we had to read them out to the group, and somehow in their verbal expression the words became much more powerful. When I started reading them I was OK – a young innocent girl in tune with nature tending her goats in the fields, her only 'sin' being to commune directly with God; she was out of tune with society and the bigoted beliefs of the day. However, as it reached the point where I was surrounded by this mob, powerful gut-wrenching sobs started to come up. My whole body shook with the force of the emotion. I had brought the powerful echo of that moment into this incarnation.

In astrological and numerological readings, I had been told of the powerful energy I carried, and I found this very difficult to believe as it was not something I had ever felt consciously. I knew I had carried a lot of anger over the years but most of that time I felt disempowered, small, timid, fearful, and in many of the early groups I joined I would find it very difficult to say anything. I just seemed to freeze up inside and my mind would go blank. What I had not known was that I had been carrying a powerful rage but I had damped it down and suppressed it because it frightened me so much. I remember an incident when I was staying with a cousin at his house when I was about thirteen years old and he was a year older. After a few weeks, we were barely tolerating each other. On the final day, I was sitting alone in the front room reading when he came in with his friend. Obviously, he was annoyed to see me and wanted me to leave, so he came to stand in front of my chair and started to call me names and harangue me (again!). My next memory is of him lying on the floor with me kneeling on top of him, thumping him. I then ran out of the room. What terrified me most was that I had no memory of how I got from sitting in the chair to kneeling on top of him on the floor.

For my next piece of writing or 'poem', please bear in mind that I had never been able to shout out when I needed to. While I was watching, my four-year-old son had walked out of his depth in the sea and went under. I was running desperately down the beach towards where I had last seen him. There were people already in the sea but they had their backs to him. I tried to shout 'Help!' so that they would notice him, but couldn't get the word louder than a whisper. He went under three times before I reached him and pulled him out. His first words were, 'God's not nice' – which surprised me, as we weren't at all religious.

Another time, many years later I had got up in the middle of the night to make myself a drink and caught my dressing gown on the gas jet, which set it alight. With the flames starting to spread, I tried to shout for my husband, but nothing but a barely audible, thin, reedy sound came out! Also bear in mind that at the beginning of the course, it had been suggested that I try shouting and banging at home because I was having so much difficulty expressing my anger. I waited till the house was empty, went to the very centre of the (detached) house for fear of the neighbours hearing, and still could not do it!

Now that the terrified part of me, my inner child, was out in the open and she (I) had become more confident, there began to arise a sense of injustice as to what had happened all those long years ago, represented by a rising anger.

During these final few days in the group, someone had said something to me that had felt like she had stuck a knife in me. She had the same defence pattern as my mother, controlling either by overpowering or undermining. Finally I could no longer contain this sort of treatment. I remember my first words were, 'I can't contain this, I can't contain this.' This time I did not collapse inwards and I was able to challenge the woman over what she had said, and a confrontation between us began. However, I remember very little after that. I have no idea what I was saying to her and what she was replying. I appeared to be outside of my consciousness. I had only flashes of awareness now and then. The rage had taken over completely.

Afterwards I was told (and had the bruises to show for it) that I was banging on the wooden arms of the chair I was sitting in to emphasise what I was saying. I was told I kept physically collapsing forward (bending over) and the facilitator needed to push me upright so that I could continue. When I collapsed forwards, the anger was compressed down. When I sat upright, it was enabled to continue rising up and out. I was mirroring how I had spent my childhood and beyond, 'collapsing' down into myself and so compressing the anger within – hence the depressions.

I do have a memory that at one point she leaned towards me screaming, 'I hate you!' and I saw that word 'hate' on the screen of my mind's eye. I remember forcing it back out of my mind, clearing the screen, by literally leaning forwards and with my hands 'pushed away' her hate, saying, 'That's your shit, this is my shit.'

In other words, I was not taking on board her emotions and opinions at the expense of my own, not going to allow her 'hate' to overwhelm me and blot out my own. We were each responsible for our own, and for the first time I was going to stay with my own stuff, express what was in me.

The next memory is that I leaned forward and shouted, 'I hate you!' back. It began as a shout but changed into a roar – a roar of pure rage – an elemental sound I had never before made and never will again. In that instance I saw those three people who had brought me up – my mother, father and great-grandmother – and knew this roar of outrage was directed at them. It had nothing to do with this person, in this group, in this moment. They had only been the trigger for me to express the rage that I had been carrying for so many years.

The Road to Healing

I then needed to re-experience all those emotions that
  I had felt as a child –
But had successfully buried under anger and depression.
The fear of these emotions had held me in a grip of
  paralysis all my life,
Doing everything I could to protect myself against
  ever feeling them again.

Because it was only in the reliving of these terrifying
  feelings and emotions,
And the learning that I would not be destroyed by
  them,
That I could start the process of becoming fully alive.

But first needed to be uttered the rage of childhood
Finally allowed to see the light of day,
An existential roar at the outrage
That life in the form of grown-ups
Had perpetrated on me as a child
That is perpetrated on all young children,
On all young souls,

A cry against the powerlessness and pain of 'growing
  up',
A roar at the Universe,
For all the hurt and unfairness and silent suffering –
It was the roar of a tigress;
It was the roar of my power finally unleashed.

Interestingly I had had a session a few months back with my hypnotherapist. Hypnotherapy is all about visualisations or inner journeys, often travelling back into childhood or into an emotion. This particular visualisation found me lowering myself into the darkness of depression. I went into that black, suffocating space but after a while discovered that underneath was an inferno and my initial reaction was fear. With trepidation, I let myself drop into the flames and to be in the flames; then to my great surprise I dropped through on to a sandy beach in front of a blue sea, where everything was still, cool, calm and at peace. I realised now the flames beneath the darkness was the rage, but beneath the rage, beneath all the emotions, there was the still, calm core of me.

Not everyone will 'roar' out in this way – we are all different energy types. Maybe you are a gentle dormouse, who will whimper out its sadness and hurt. In a counselling session, one client was able to touch on some deep inner pain that despite years of counselling had remained hidden. When she got home and was relaying it to her partner, she suddenly started sobbing uncontrollably – she said, 'like a child cries'. She had at last found her inner child. It was her birthday two days later, and her children were singing 'Happy Birthday' to her, and she found herself laughing and giggling 'just like a child'. In fact, she made them keep singing it over and over, she was enjoying it so much. As a child she had never had her birthday celebrated (even though her siblings had), and as an adult had found this day intensely uncomfortable; but now for the first time she and her inner child could thoroughly enjoy their 'first' birthday together.

Another client felt she was nearly there, but there seemed to be one final block. She was by now very in touch with her body and she felt/sensed that there was a large tangled 'knot' inside her womb that she couldn't get rid of. When she had first become aware of it, it had seemed too frightening and painful to get anywhere near it. This time she was able to visualise herself finally entering into the knotted ball, and inside she found her inner child. She was able to untangle her child and, after reassurance, coaxed her to come out – at which point we realised her inner child was hungry! As she had always had weight problems, she suddenly realised that she had unknowingly been trying to 'feed' her child but because she was hidden inside her safe 'prison', the 'food' had not been getting through to her. She had tried to assuage her child's hunger for nourishment by eating and eating, and ended up overweight. From then on she was able to control her appetite and stop putting on weight, as now she was able to meet the needs of her inner child directly.

Or it may be a slow, gentle, ongoing process of awakening. One client started coming to me because she was depressed and couldn't shake off the symptoms. She came regularly for over two years and just talked and talked as she tried to make sense of her feelings and reactions to her family and friends. Slowly but surely she began to reclaim her power, so that when she was put down by her family, she began to recover more quickly. The depression symptoms began to lessen and disappear. The more she understood the more aware she became; the more she recovered her different selves the nearer she got to her inner child. There came the day when she was no longer upset by being put down. She remained on balance and centred because her child knew now that she was loved and would be taken care of.

Or maybe you will experience it as a shift of energy – a surge that runs through your whole being, through all your physical, emotional and mental levels at once, as though the trapped energy is bursting through a huge dam that had been holding it in.

Or you might be someone who regularly meditates maybe two or three times a day, which in turn helps you to become more aware of your inner being, which enables you to sit with each feeling and emotion that arises until they release organically. However it releases, trust that it is right for you.

I was fortunate to be able to reach the stage in my process when I was able to break through all the blockages and finally connect with my personal power. My mother wasn't. A Leo, she was potentially a powerful woman, but that power was snarled up, suffocated, forced down beneath dark depression. Her power simmered inside of her with no outlet, so it leaked out in her harangues and her outbursts, rather like a pressure cooker when the steam will suddenly hiss out. My mother's emotions were intense. And so were mine. I thought this was how it was, but realise not all people experience emotions to such a degree. We are all different. I looked up the meaning of 'intense' and the dictionary states, 'existing in a high degree, violent, vehement; having some quality in high degree'. I asked a couple of my class what this word 'intense' meant to them, and they both thought of it as negative as they were not comfortable around it. The dictionary also says 'eager, ardent', so that intensity can be a positive force. Yet the word 'force' in itself holds a power. It is not gentle. (To clarify, I am talking 'emotion' here, not feeling. There is a difference between the two which I explain later.)

Codependency

Have you ever felt drained after spending time with someone? It could be that person is an energy 'vampire', that is someone who feels better by taking energy from another. My mother used me from a very early age as a repository for all her emotional outpourings, all her secrets, fears, anger, bitterness, resentments, blame, hopes, dreams. She fed off my energy to make herself feel better. At its height it was so extreme I was subsumed by her. In later years I learned how the body shows us very clearly what our emotional problems are (as within, so without) and so I came to understand why, during those final years I was trapped in that room with my mother, I had a tapeworm. It was highlighting the parasitic effect my mother's energy was having on me. I had a parasite taking my energy, feeding off me, draining me and that parasite was both inside and outside my body. (I still squirm at the thought!)

However, we can collude in this. It's not necessarily one way if we allow it to happen. It becomes a two-way process. I grew up believing there was only one way for me to behave in relationships – to be the listener. It felt good if the other felt better after talking to me. I had developed a need to be needed and I was therefore colluding in the energy drain. As a result codependence develops.

For many years I felt a lot of guilt at the way I had brought up my daughter, who was now developing the family trait of depression and anxiety and, like my mother, was emotionally dependent on me, pouring out all the pain, anger and worry on me. I felt I owed it to her to be there for her. Eventually I began to understand the codependency we (my mother, my daughter and I) had in our relationships, and the need to cut the cords of emotional attachment to free up each of us, so that we were no longer leaning on each other.

Feeding Off Me

Feeding off me,
Holding on to me,
Draining my energy –

The only way for my mother to feel better,
The only way for my daughter to get by.
They did not have their own resources
And drank from my energy well to survive.

I escaped from the first, ran away,
Built great walls and barriers to keep her out,
And she kept knocking and crying
And threatening to be let back in,
But I only lowered the drawbridge when she was
    dying.

With the second I stood my ground and said no more
And yet I have resurrected no walls, no barriers
I am still here, waiting
For when my daughter is ready
To stand before me in her own light.

With my daughter, I kept having this vision that she was dangling over the edge of an abyss and I was leaning over holding on to her hand and if I didn't hold on, she would fall and be lost for ever. I was the only one who could stop her disappearing for ever into the abyss. Maybe this dread was my own inner fear for my inner child, my soul essence. Or maybe it was the very real suicide attempts my mother made, and being told by her I was the only one who was keeping her alive. However, the more I grew and developed the more it became increasingly draining for me to listen to my daughter's outpourings, especially if I was already an empty vessel, drained of all energy, because of my own process. On one such occasion I found myself terminating the telephone call before she was ready, saying I could not cope with this right now. The guilt and dread I then experienced were huge, and I wrote the following to help me cope with the feelings and to find some reassurance that she would be all right.

CUTTING THE CORD

Tonight I could no longer listen,
I have left her to fend for herself.
I had to let go, and this has now been done.
It had to be done, I know,
And I am trying not to think of her
In that lonely space without support.

I know she is being held
But it is unseen by her
And she thinks she has no one.

But it was at my expense
And I can no longer pay the price:
In the saving of myself
I am also freeing her
Because she has to learn to fly.

She does not know it yet,
But she is now flying on her own.
Soon she will learn how to soar,
Nearer and nearer the Light.

She is protected by Light,
Surrounded by loving Helpers
They will look after her.

Her Soul will know
What I have done and why,
And it will understand.
Her light will shine forth, bright and true,
A beacon for the Heavens to see
And she will slowly become a channel
Through which the light of love will pass
And then she will be free.

And these years later? She stands before me in her own light just as predicted in my previous writing. (Phew!)

She has since discovered that at the soul level I had contracted to support her in this lifetime until she secured her own foundation. (It all works perfectly!)

My mother died in 1992. In the last three months she was dying, I went up regularly. I was the only one left. She had pushed everyone else away – family, friends, neighbours – and my father had died twelve years earlier. He had been an invalid his last seven years and my mother his carer, a role she relished, as she felt needed. I think they were closer during that time than they had ever been. After his death I had tried to support her as much as possible, but kept her at a distance emotionally. I phoned her regularly, visited more often, sorted out any problems she might have (such as getting her moved into sheltered accommodation). Often when I did visit her I would try to take someone with me so that she would not turn on me – I was in my forties and still afraid of her! Even so I would end up the day in a foetal-like huddle in the chair, feeling bombarded and sucked dry!

In these final months I went back into the spider's web, allowing her to have expectations of me once again, letting down the emotional walls and reconnecting. A lot of fear came up that I would be for ever trapped if she didn't die. I went up each weekend – 'My daughter a carer – who would have thought?' This had been *her* role in life. She had nursed her grandmother and her husband, both of them for long years. She had worked in a hospital and been a home help. Being a carer had been her badge of pride.

Towards the end I have a vivid memory of speaking to one of the hospital care workers who told me they were arranging to transfer her into a hospice. She told me that my mother had said she would go home (she could be very stubborn), and when asked how she would manage had replied that I would have to go to look after her. The word she used to describe my mother in that moment was 'intimidating'. She had been quite taken aback by the force of my mother's words. I remember thinking, *At last, confirmation as to what it had been like!* In the event, she was too ill to go home and died some weeks later.

Before she died I told her what she needed to hear, that she was loved. I wanted her to hear this; she had not been told the words often during her lifetime. When she died, we went to sit with the body, and I was able to glimpse her soul, a divine spark once again, with two others on either side of her. I knew she was being looked after. Finally.

SEARCHING FOR ANSWERS

I was doing a lot of intuitive writing now, trying to understand the various parts of me that were currently seeking expression, searching for ways in which to come to terms with all the various feelings arising. I was learning that we needed first to accept all our feelings, even the negative ones, so that we could then let them go. I was aware of a lot of my negative side but had very little idea of what my positives were. I had no idea I was compassionate until my therapist told me, and I was fifty-five at the time! She asked me, 'What quality do you have in spades?' and I answered, 'Logic.'

She had been thinking of compassion. I was surprised; I had no idea it was one of my qualities. (I went to a hypnotherapist for a year when I was doing my counsellor training, to help me contain and make sense of everything that was coming up. She was amazing, quite unconventional at times, but she gave me the insights I needed.)

However, realising and then accepting, for example, that I had an impatient side to me, often did not help me to handle the feelings well. How could I let them go when they seemed to come out of nowhere when I was least expecting it? *Why am I so impatient?* my rational, analytical mind queried as it tried, yet again, to solve the problem!

IMPATIENCE

> I am impatience and
> I yearn for clarity and understanding,
> Direct and open communication.
> When I am not understood
> I am frustrated because I feel isolated,
> A voice in the wilderness, no one hearing me.

So take a deep breath, slow down, take time,
Acknowledge your frustration and allow it to fade.

The impatience rises in me
When others fail to see me,
To value me and my thoughts.
They underestimate me and my meaning,
They do not listen to what I am struggling to impart.

So take a deep breath, slow down, take time,
Speak your truth carefully, whether or not it is heard.

The frustration rises in me
When I fail to find words to explain what I mean.
The idea is there, the vision, the insight –
But the words are slow in forming to express this.

So take a deep breath, slow down, take time,
Speak your truth fearlessly and clarity will come.

What I learned eventually was that feelings are not emotions. A feeling is energy, an emotion is that energy expanding and whooshing around the body until your whole body is filled with it, until you have become that emotion. Once a feeling becomes an emotion, you have lost control of it as it is now on the move out of the solar plexus or heart centre up through your body until either it bursts from you or, if it doesn't get past the throat, it floods your body until it lodges in yet another unexpressed blockage. However, when I recovered my inner child, when I connected with that deepest part of me, I connected also with my aware self or adult self, the watcher or observer deep within that is the real me. This means that I have a part of me that is aware when a feeling does occur (it's as though it's watching it) and in that moment of awareness there is created an almost infinitesimal pause, which gives me time to catch the feeling before it changes into an emotion. In this way I am able simply to acknowledge, accept and honour it. If the feeling is at all negative or inappropriate, then I have the time in which to change the feeling to something more constructive and positive. I have a *choice*. That infinitesimal pause gives me time to choose to change my feeling of impatience into acceptance, or to change the feeling of anger into compassion and forgiveness.

I had a chronic lack of confidence. It connected to my deep-seated feeling of not being good enough. In fact, I had been told it was pathological, meaning no matter how much I worked on myself I could not get rid of it; instead it would need healing. It was so deep seated it was karmic in origin. Many of us on Earth today have brought this trait in with us, a leftover from our failure in Atlantis when we embraced the Golden Age and then squandered it. We weren't 'good enough'. However, during most of those years I did not present as timid and fearful. I received a letter just recently from a boss who had gone to prison twenty years ago, as a result of which we lost our jobs. I think he was feeling guilty about that and he wrote to us all about it. I wrote reassuring him saying it had done me a good turn, because it had brought me face to face with my lack of confidence. He replied saying 'I was totally unaware that you ever suffered a "lack of confidence". It was because you showed justifiable confidence that I wanted you to qualify…!' Even in my forties, I was not allowing how I felt to show through. I was still presenting that 'indifferent' face to the world, as my mother interpreted it.

Confidence

My confidence can desert me at any moment.
So where does it go?
It flees to safety, leaving behind a mass of fear and
 uncertainty,
Because if I hide, then nothing can get to me.

If I remain to face whatever is to come,
Then I need to be present, aware of whatever
 happens,
Feeling everything.

> Calmness is the key –
> But how to remain calm in the midst of new energies, in the eye of the storm?
> That is the answer – to be in the eye of the storm, whatever is happening,
> To be safe in the centre of me, present and aware but impregnable.

Sometimes I wrote to relieve discomfort. Waiting many feet underground on the airless platform, feeling trapped in dense, heavy energy that weighed down on me almost physically, I wrote to pass the time and to take my mind off how I was feeling.

SOUTH KENSINGTON TUBE STATION

> Waiting for the tube on a London platform
> Watching people go by,
> Strangers with the common goal
> Of rushing to be elsewhere.
>
> Obstacles strew my journey
> Delaying me, testing my patience,
> Finally stopping me, and so I sit and stare,
> Content for the moment just to be.
>
> I look more closely, more deeply
> And realise this moment is telling me
> To take more time, there's no need to push –
> Slow down, take it easy, look around –
> And I see beautiful souls going by.

I was becoming much more aware, feeling more whole (no longer a big, black hole inside me), able to relate better to others, in touch with all my feelings, yet still had days when I felt disconnected and lonely. I had a tendency to beat myself up because I was allowing myself to feel like this yet again. Hadn't I learned yet? I 'should' not be feeling like this. Why wasn't I more disciplined? I 'should' be meditating, making positive affirmations, walking in nature, exercising. I was still not good enough. It was taking me a long while to release these old, deeply ingrained patterns.

Down

I am feeling down
And this feeling leads me to cessation,
There is nothing I can think of that I want to do,
There is nothing I can settle to, to make the feeling go away.

I want to hide in fantasy
Not think of the emptiness I feel inside, the realisation again that I feel bored,
That I have lost that inner connection that makes me feel alive.

How to lift the spirit?
There is no spirit present to lift, that is how it feels,
I have lost touch with it, I have lost touch with Who I Am.

It leaves a gaping hole
A boredom, a frustration, an aimlessness, a resignation,
A repugnance that I have allowed this to happen yet again.

Too stretched out,
Too taut to relax, which is when I need to relax the most,
And knowing this makes me feel even worse.

How was I to grow beyond this feeling of being stuck that was plaguing me? One moment I felt so alive, so hopeful, and yet the next I had lost it all again. I wrote to find the answers. It helped to clear the fog, to reach through to that still, calm voice within, to find the answers. I had not realised until now how much my path was one of being alone rather than being surrounded by people all the time. I learned how much I needed *personal space* in which to come back to centre, to rebalance my energies, to rest and relax, to calm my mind and emotions – to get back to me.

In the Doldrums

I am in the doldrums, too off balance,
Too much time spent working and thinking of work,
Too much time with other people surrounded by
    their energies,
Too little space to recover.

I have descended into greyness,
Overtired, overstressed,
More stretched out, a taut wire quivering,
And my balance is destroyed.

Slow down, walk in nature, sit in the garden,
And you regain your balance, your calm, your centre.

In a Dark Tunnel

The future is not yet revealed,
It hides behind a veil,
The present is all I see.
The past has fashioned me,
What I see now is coloured
By what I have become.

Yet the present is dark, tiring and foggy,
So I strain to see beyond the veil.
Yet the more I strain,
The more stuck I become,
The more I weary myself.

> Stop trying;
> You only exhaust yourself.
> Allow the fog, the darkness;
> Know that the seeds are growing within.

Trust has been especially difficult for me to embrace. I have spent most of my years worrying about the past, the present and the future. I would agonise for long periods over something someone said or did; I would be unable to make a decision because it might not be the right one; I would worry and fret over what might or might not happen in the future. I discovered I had a deep-seated belief that I could not trust anyone because they would end up betraying me. I have memories of many playground relationships, when a friend would go off with someone else and they'd turn their backs on me. For years I felt insecure in many friendships not realising it was because of my unconscious fear that they would eventually reject or betray me. This belief contributed to my marriage breakdown. (It's our beliefs that create our reality, which is why we need to reprogram our subconscious – the repository of all the negative, fearful beliefs we have brought with us from childhood.)

Slowly, trust was creeping in. I was beginning to reveal myself. I was relying more on my intuition. I was finding I could trust others, especially as I was becoming more accepting of them. However, I still needed to learn to go with the flow, trusting that all was unfolding perfectly.

TRUST

> Trust that you are nearing your goal;
> Trust every day;
> Trust that I am with you
> Every step of the way.
>
> Lift up your eyes and see Me
> In the raindrop
> In the sunshine,
> In the dew on a rose petal.

> Be aware of Me
> In every breath you take;
> In every thought you have;
> In every atom dancing its life force.
>
> Lift up your face to the Light
> And in trust, stride forward –
> Moving into your higher purpose,
> Stepping into your true potential.

At one point, I kept picking angel cards with the words 'Sisterhood/Brotherhood' and did not understand the meaning. I was an only child, had had difficulty much of my life reaching out to others, of feeling I belonged in any group situation, so was trying to understand the concept when I wrote the following:

SISTERHOOD/BROTHERHOOD

> Sisters, brothers, sharing common ground,
> Sharing a bond deeper than friendship,
> An unspoken bond of loyalty – a union, a family.
>
> Part of a whole, from the same source,
> Many group together, unquestioning reliance on each other,
> Helping each other in times of need,
> Ready to share their burden if it becomes too much
>
> Too long on my own, time to come out...
> Join the Sisterhood, be a part of the Brotherhood,
> Enjoy the feeling of belonging, of sharing, of uniting.

Another important step was to try to express my feelings. Not the emotions, like my mother was so good at throwing out, but each gentle feeling as it arose. Even anger can be gentle when it is just a feeling – awareness of a 'pang' in the solar plexus, and a calm 'I feel anger at that'. Unfortunately, I don't always know what I'm feeling in the moment, so I learned to say, 'I don't feel comfortable,' or, 'I've had a reaction.' As I progressed, it became 'a part of me is' or 'my inner child is'. If I stop and try to define the feeling first, then I've distanced myself from the feeling by going into my head, which was my old pattern. Understanding what the feeling is comes sooner or later, but it is important to attempt some sort of expression of it in the moment, as this will prevent any energy attaching to it and taking it out of your control or leaving it to fester.

Sometimes being very spiritual does not necessarily mean that a person's psychological awareness is equally advanced. I knew of a very spiritual person who had a really beautiful energy, yet when she became angry, she confronted the other person and flung at them the negative energy of the *emotion* rather than a calm expression of the *feeling*. She allowed her anger to overwhelm her. She called this 'speaking her truth', but all people heard was the emotion, the energy, behind her words, and her valid points were lost. She was speaking her truth at the level of awareness she was at. If she had never been able to speak out before, then this was a big step forward for her. However, like all of us, she still had work to do to increase her level of awareness, her level of consciousness. Speak from your calm centre, from your heart, and you will be heard. It might not always be apparent that you have been heard, but on an energetic or unconscious level you will be.

CONNECTING WITH PLANET EARTH

I completed the training course in 1997 but it had taken a lot of out of me. I had gone through an intense personal change and it had taken its toll on my health. It felt as though I had burnt out. I was not sleeping and could not digest food properly. I was exhausted. I was so drained of energy I could not go into a supermarket or any place where there were a lot of people. If I did, it was as though all the energy in there was physically pressing down on me, and my body would start to ache. All those locked away feelings and emotions were coming to the surface. I felt raw and vulnerable, as though I had just been born. I needed time to recover from the 'birth trauma' and to get used to this new way of being. I stopped working for a few months. I started seeing a naturopath. Slowly I went about the task of recovering. It felt like I needed to recuperate. I rested. I nurtured myself. It took over a year. I was changed in all sorts of ways, not just emotionally but on all levels. I was now a vegetarian and food combined.* I slept much less than I used to. I spent a lot of time on my own. I preferred to be out in the country rather than in the centre of a city. My awareness and sensitivity had increased.

RECOVERY

It felt that for so long I had been stumbling through a
dark tunnel with no light at the end.
Then there came a glimmer of light at the end of the
tunnel, and
Suddenly I was out of the tunnel, walking in a deep
ditch with high banks either side,
Trying to lift each foot out of the sticky, clinging mud
that I was wading through.
Then came the time when I finally realised I had
climbed up to the top of the bank,
The path was dry and solid beneath my feet but I was
still covered with mud,
And needed to stand awhile while I dried out and
cleaned off.

As the mud dried and fell off, I began to see
That I was surrounded by summer blossom, bird-
song, green foliage and blue skies
And my heart swelled with hope and joy as I realised I
could walk freely and easily.
I set off once more down my path, walking into a
light-filled future.

My eyes were opening. We see through the lens of our level of consciousness. If we are not very aware, our vision is limited. I was seeing more clearly than ever before. It seemed so fresh and light. I was much more aware of everything around me, appreci-

---

* Eating protein with vegetables at one meal and carbohydrates with vegetables at another. The combination of protein and carbohydrates was too heavy or acidic for my, by now, sensitive digestion.

ating each moment. This is a memory of a summer Sunday in Somerset (I like the alliteration!). On holiday, we were taking these walks on our way to a pub lunch.

IN THE COUNTRYSIDE

We walked today by the River Brue
Through the fields of buttercups and clover,
Long waving grasses, sturdy cow parsley.

Up and over stiles,
Through bushes and brambles, cascading wild roses,
Trees shading the water,
A barrier of nettles – a farmer's revenge.

The sun was shining in the bright blue sky,
A breeze blowing, shaking the trees and cooling the skin.

A horse dozed in the shade of a tree,
A dog from the farm followed us in friendship,
The bullocks from curiosity followed us with purpose.

Birds in the hedgerows were singing and chatting
While a dog on the opposite bank bravely told us off.

The river rippled by quiet in the summer sun,
Electric blue damselflies dancing and winging across the water.

A time to remember, a time to treasure.

It was as though I was noticing all of this with new eyes. It was as though I was seeing it all as a child would see it. Remember the look of wonder on a small child's face when it sees a buttercup for the first time. While playing in the fields as a child I have many memories of examining all the different wild flowers, being aware of all the colours, textures and scents. I lost all that as I grew older but it was all coming back. I was revelling in this reconnection to the Earth, and at the same time I was grounding myself.

Another View of the Same Walk

>The wind blowing the trees sounding huge orchestral notes,
>The leaves swaying in the willows, a silver grey ballet of movement.
>
>The river winding along sometimes flowing, sometimes still,
>The swans drifting on a bend, white and alert and emotionless.
>
>The stiles in different sizes, precarious when old and rickety,
>The attention fixed on clambering over safely,
>Interesting when new and sturdy,
>The anticipation set on what lay ahead.
>
>The greeting from the old Shire horse
>As he ambled over to see what intruded,
>His field cropped neat and green, a contrast to the next,
>Where nettles and brambles challenge the way.
>
>Befriended by the black collie from the farm,
>Bounding ahead on the path
>Living in the moment, full of love and bonhomie to all,
>Except for the cat running for cover.
>
>The many-barred gate to be climbed over,
>Speedily when the bullocks become curious,
>Adrenalin lending agility to old bones;
>Resting afterwards on the gnarled old log,
>Eyeballing the bullocks clustered at the gate:
>Well-being and contentment the result
>As the sun continued to shine.

I'd had difficulty up to now finding my way to new places on my own. Probably my lack of confidence played a part in this. Maybe I was still carrying that dread I felt at sixteen when I didn't know what bus to catch and my mother was too dazed to help. Going out of my comfort zone had brought up a lot of fears over the years. Now I was pushing those restrictive barriers out, and one summer I began exploring further afield. On my own I would drive out into the countryside, finding new walks in woods or over fields. The more I did this, the more an incredible sense of freedom was arising in me. The more I saw and appreciated the beauty of Mother Nature, the more gratitude and thankfulness welled up in me. The more I felt better about myself, the more my sense of inner freedom grew. The freer I became, the more I connected with a sense of deep joy, humility and reverence. My heart was truly opening.

On these walks I began to access moments of stillness, when I would tune in to the peace all around. In those moments I was fully present, my mind still, my emotions calm. I would be aware at a very deep level of the beauty I found myself in, of the sheer pleasure of being alive in such life-enhancing surroundings.

Penn Woods

Sitting in the woods, the sun on high,
The knobbly bark of the tree I am leaning against
The lace pattern of leaves against the clear sky.

Butterflies darting to and fro among the grasses and ferns,
Glorious greens of every hue sparkle and shine and calm the eye.

So quiet, a fly buzzing by is the only sound,
Save for the breeze rustling in the trees.

> I sit in the shade of a birch tree and watch the warmth
> of the sun,
> Aware of the stillness and peace
> Supremely content, glad to be alive, and oh, so thankful!

The kids had by now all flown the nests. When the last child left, we 'upsized' as opposed to downsized. We bought a larger house so that we could each have plenty of space. Therefore, although still working, when I was at home I was now able to have the time I needed to be on my own, the time to rebalance and come back to centre, to contemplate, to study, to write – all the things that it was in my nature to do, rather than the frantic socialising I had been doing in the 1970s and '80s. I was moving into my energetic potential, accepting who I was and finding out what I needed. The following was written as I sat in my garden one summer's day, leaning against my favourite apple tree.

SITTING IN THE GARDEN

> The sky high and blue
> Leaning against the apple tree,
> Gentle breeze caressing skin and
> Rustling the leaves overhead.
>
> Bare feet on cool grass,
> Smooth, newly mown lawn,
> Bright with sunlight
> Patterned with tree shadows.
>
> Watching ants hurrying by
> And magpies strutting,
> A pigeon waiting for food.
>
> The red tiled roof framed by trees very tall,
> Apples and pears weighing down branches.

A kaleidoscope of colour, orange flame,
White marguerites, red fuchsia and pink hydrangea.

A sense of peace and calm,
The stillness of a summer day.

To be able to share such a moment with my husband and to appreciate his presence in my life was also a beautiful experience, as when we were walking in Essex one day.

STURGEON'S WALK

The sun shining as we walk through the golden fields
Until finally we lean against the fence, resting,
Watching the sheep grazing, the horses in the next field.
Time to stop, to appreciate Nature and to be.

The warmth of the sun enhancing the stillness of the day,
Flies and bees buzzing by, birds singing,
Distant sounds of traffic and tractor,
Contentment in the moment and in the companionship of each other.

Beauty can be found in man-made structures, not just in Nature. Even going into the centre of a great town could now bring its insights and connections for me. Inner stillness can be carried anywhere, although I admit it's sometimes difficult not to feel overwhelmed when surrounded by a mass of energies. I remember meeting my by now grown-up daughter in London, who was also on a similar personal and spiritual development path.

A Meeting in London

In the centre of a great cosmopolitan city
A seething, teeming metropolis
We came together for a few short hours.

Amid the hustle and bustle, the raw chaotic energy,
An oasis of calm and connection,
A bright spark of awareness, lighting up the darkness.

More and more these sparks are burning, steadily and joyfully,
For they know that the Light that flows through them
Is the Light of mankind's future –
One filled with hope and joy, peace and love.

My Path

Like you, I am a soul who has taken on a physical form in which to experience life on Earth. I have come here to re-experience and release all the negativity I had been carrying, in order that I could open up to who I really was, an eternal soul in human form, a part of All That Is. We bring our karma in with us. It is imprinted in us as sub-personalities, negative traits and blockages, which need to be uncovered and released. We are then free to move into a higher dimension of reality.

When we incarnate, most of us go through a period of believing and feeling that we have disconnected from Source. However, this is not so, and our task is to *realise* this. Self-realisation is about getting to know ourselves, not just on a mental level but also at the *experiential* level. In other words, the knowing, the realisation includes how it *feels* to be ourselves, first at the personality level and then at the soul level.

Initially I did not link the meditation and spiritual exploration with the personality work I was doing. It took some years before it all came together – the realisation that each part of me was linked, it was all me. I did a five-day intensive based on a Zen satori, where we sat in pairs and, while the other listened, tried to find our way to an answer of the question we had been given to work on. It's like a verbal meditation. Then we would change and listen while our partner worked on their koan – just listening, no responses. After a while we would change partners and start again and so it went on for the whole day. Koans are paradoxical questions designed to open the mind, to enlighten. The first question I pondered was, 'Who am I?' After one and half days I reached the conclusion that 'I am me and I am part of the Whole and the Whole is part of me'.

The following was the first piece of intuitive writing I did, started while sitting on the Tube station and continued on the train itself. The words just flowed out, much to my surprise and joy.

I AM

I am the Sun that shines,
The Rain that follows.

I am the Rose that blooms,
The Thorn that warns.

I am the Fruit that ripens,
The Seed that falls.

I am the Thought that illumines,
The Emotion that drowns.

I am the Spirit that soars,
The Body that grounds.

I am Earth and Fire,
Water and Air.

I am Light and Dark,
Sound and Silence.

I am Yin and I am Yang,

I am the atom in the Universe,
And the Universe is but an atom within me.

I Am.

The more I grew and developed, meditated and walked in nature, and took time out for myself to regroup my energies, the more I became aware of my intuitive flashes. I am very visual and my intuition comes to me on the screen of my third eye, where I might see an image or a word, both accompanied by a sense of knowing. I was also using the intuitive writing as a way of accessing my inner guidance.

The Inner Guide

I am here to help you, to guide and assist you,
I am wise beyond compare
And know what you need, and when and where –
You may not have noticed me but my messages are
    there.

You can see me or hear me, you can feel me or sense
    me
But first, be still,
Relax your body, calm your emotions, clear your
    thoughts
And in the silence, in the stillness, there I am.

I was reading everything I could lay my hands on about the spiritual journey. I was attending courses and workshops. I was a member of a regular meditation group. Feelings of excitement led me on to try that, learn this, experience the other. At times it was mind-blowing. I felt I was emerging from a long, dark tunnel.

How Far Have I Come?

Much of my life so far has the feel of a painful journey through a dark swamp of emotional silt,
At times, thrashing around in anger, often just frozen in hopelessness, sometimes nearly going under,
Moving slowing and painfully forward, wading through a sea of mud, heavy slow fumbling steps,
Dark lowering clouds pressing all around,
The darkness often blurred and blotted out by an alcohol and drug-induced numbness,
The brief glimpses of blue sky too soon slipping from my grasp.

But a growing spiritual awareness has given me a purpose and the strength
To wean myself of my addictive props and to lay bare my emotional turmoil,
Exploring the depths in all their rawness, locating the terror so long locked away
And surviving, my lost child reclaimed, my aware wise woman in place.

A period of exhaustion and rest, not knowing what to do or where to go…

But now the feeling of purpose again, as though I am scrambling up the banks,
Out of that swamp on to firmer ground, struggling to stand up and brush myself down,
Thinking about how to take my first tentative steps down the road that stretches before me.

I am revelling in feelings not often felt before, of well-being and contentment, of a sense of freedom,
The sense of starting an exciting journey full of new things to learn, new sounds and sights to experience.

> I want to be a wise woman, a teacher, a prophetess,
> not just the frightened child I sometimes am.
> I want to be full of light always, not just now and
> again.
>
> To feel centred is my aim, to let it be a way of life, to
> live in the here and now,
> Contented with the moment, trusting of the next
> moment.
>
> For only in balance do I find calm and peace, am I
> fully aware, do I feel the joy of living
> And in this centeredness I raise up my eyes to give
> thanks that I am now fully alive,
> To give thanks for the protection and help I have
> received, and to give thanks for the beauty that I see
> before me.

I started to learn about Lightworkers (someone who is consciously aware of working with the Light) and how they have a dual purpose. I was here not only for my own process of self-discovery, growth and development (ascension, in fact) but also to help others along their way. This was the reason I had had these urges over the years to be of service. How was my world service going to manifest? What were my gifts? What was my passion? Having been in offices all my working life (as secretary, bookkeeper, legal executive, personal assistant, housing officer, administrator), I was more than surprised to be told that I was here as a *teacher*. In fact, a few more years passed before I started to create and then run courses on personal and spiritual awakening – again, much to my surprise.

When I am counselling or taking a class, I call upon my guide before I begin and know that, when needed, answers will be provided and the teaching will be suited to this particular class. I work with my guides intuitively rather than psychically, and have learned to trust my sense of knowing when in the midst of counselling or teaching. This trust built up with practise. When I first started teaching and someone asked me a question, I would sometimes find myself replying, 'I don't know,' and then hear myself going on to provide that very answer. My personality self didn't know the answer but my guide, my inner wisdom, my connection to the Universal Mind (whatever you want to call it) did. In one particular instance, I remember watching myself as this was happening. Part of me was saying, 'I've no idea what I'm going to say next,' and I would continue talking – it was as though I was reading it off my third eye screen.

My energies have so far been more focused on teaching. However, when I do have a client for counselling, I find I attract those who are already spiritually aware and have a need to go deep within, to the very core of their being.

My Path

Mine is a path of study and learning,
To experience, to analyse and so to understand.

Mine is a path of personal and spiritual growth,
Shaking off the bonds and hurts of childhood,
Embracing the remembered wisdom of the Soul.

And now the fire within burns bright and true
To impart this knowledge through counselling and
    teaching,
Connecting at a deep level with another
To heal their wounds and to illumine their path.

My tools are compassion and empathy, insight and
    intuition,
I channel the light of healing and illumination
Into the dark recesses of their very being
And the healing energy banishes fear and terror.

> I travel alongside them but a short time
> While I bear witness to their struggle to emerge,
> And whole again, having reclaimed their full potential,
> They continue on their journey to transcendence.
>
> And I give thanks that I have been given this privilege
> As I experience again that awe and reverence
> For that moment when the Universe stills
> And the light of compassion pours through
> To hold and comfort, to soothe and heal, to strengthen and transform.

I am a listener. I grew up watching and listening. I listened as a safety precaution. What's the mood today? Is it safe to talk? Is it safe to come out of hiding? My teens were spent listening to my mother as she spewed out all her angst. A lot of my relationships in my early years were based on my listening while they talked. I became a Samaritan and listened and began to realise that it was good to listen because often they would feel better. I could soothe just by listening. I'm told there are different levels of listening. Level One listeners don't hear you at all, they just want to talk about themselves; you might get a word in edgeways but they are busy thinking of their reply while you are talking. Level Two listeners appear to listen but miss the point, as they have no real understanding or empathy with what you are saying. A Level Three listener is really present, empathic enough to understand, yet detached enough so as not to take on your story. It's the level of a counsellor. This was now my level of listening. Honed over the years, my childhood safety precaution is now a skill I can use to help others. Although still empathic, I have learned to remain detached from the emotions of others, no longer overwhelmed as I was when young. Because I can remain detached, I'm far more in tune with my intuition, which enables me to convey and channel a higher wisdom. My gift is to enable others to see the bigger picture.

And now I talk as well. I teach, passing on the knowledge and wisdom I have gained. I communicate, expressing my feelings – no longer *I think*, rather *I feel*. In this way I am revealing who I am, no longer hiding. It's OK to be me. I'm not saying there aren't moments when the old insecurities sweep through me, the old patterns take hold of me, but they don't stay long and I soon regain my balance.

What can I say about counselling? Some are very against it. I am all for it. Counselling is not about changing who you are. It is about discovering who you are. It is about changing your relationship to yourself, the way you see yourself. There are many who are doing this without the need to have counselling. It's just one path among many paths; for we are all unique, and therefore we each walk an individual path suited to us alone.

The many hours of training I did was such an amazing journey it would take another book to detail it all. The course encompassed different models of psychotherapy and counselling, from psychoanalytic and humanistic to person-centred approaches. It also included body and energy work and 'the transpersonal and spiritual dimensions of human experience', as the brochure stated. We met for five hours in the evening once a week (part of which was an encounter group), plus weekends of art therapy, voice dialogue, psychodrama, the mother, the father, primal, gestalt, encounter – I can't remember them all now. There were five-day intensives, and on top of all this we co-counselled each other once a week. It involved us directly experiencing each technique and process. It involved us exploring ourselves so that we could embrace all the different parts of who and what we were. Each interaction brought up feelings and emotions; each experience uncovered another layer; each process sparked insight. I felt I was turned inside out until there was nothing left to hide. At the end, every part of me was there in the quivering rawness of new birth.

One experience of co-counselling remains with me. The person I was counselling was in a deep, dark space, so much so that she could not speak or express it in any way. It seemed to me that she was so disconnected that no Light could reach in to heal her. Her guides and angels were around her but she had closed off from them. Silently I visualised bringing down the Light through my crown chakra to my heart chakra, out to her and down through her. The silence deepened, my awareness heightened and there was a stillness as though time was waiting. I had a sense as if the whole of the Universe had turned its attention on to us. There was a deep sense of reverence (awe and joy) at being present in this moment. It seemed special in some way.

Eventually the session ended. When we were discussing it afterward she said she had found herself trapped in a very dark space but then she felt a very fine, gentle golden energy starting to pour into her from the top of her head and it went right down to her toes, tingling as it went. She had then sensed the still reverence of the moment. In that moment our relationship had transcended itself and become part of something larger.

We don't need to be in a formal counselling or healing session to achieve this. When our inner spirit reaches out and touches the inner spirit of another, transcendence occurs. Which is what the word Namaste is saying, one interpretation of which is, 'I honour the place in you, which is of love, of light, of truth and of peace. When you are in that place in you, and I am in that place in me, we are one.' In that moment of transcendence, we become part of the Oneness for which there are many names, such as Spirit, God, Creator, Source, All That Is, the Universal Mind, the Ultimate Cosmic Consciousness.

I found it difficult to use the word God because of my childhood experience of the word. I was brought up by a Catholic mother whose view was very traditional and childlike. I was sent to Sunday schools (both Methodist and Anglican) for many years, and was confirmed at the local parish church around the age of thirteen, alongside my friend Anne. Leading up to it, we had to go for weekly classes from the rector, who told us that when we were confirmed the Holy Spirit would enter into us. I was so looking forward to this. Dressed in our white dresses, all the proud parents in church, we knelt at the altar and I waited for the Holy Spirit to enter into me and felt... nothing. I waited for quite a few days just in case there had been a delay, you know, busy with all these other children to enter... nothing. Emptiness. I was very disappointed. I can't remember if I thought it might be my fault, not good enough and all that, but I'm sure it contributed to my later questioning and rejection of the whole concept of religion and embracing first existentialism and later humanism. It wasn't until after 1987 that I began to realise I might have thrown the baby out with the bath water! I remember using that phrase when it started to dawn on me there was so much more to this being on Earth.

The Later Years

Looking Back

By now I was aware that I was now classed as the older generation by the younger people I worked with. Often their eyes would glaze over as they tried politely to show an interest in what I was saying, when they really just wanted to relate to their own generation. They saw me as being on a par with their parents or even grandparents! In my younger years I would have been mortally offended and tried to change myself, tried to fit in, but now I just felt quietly amused – confirmation that I had indeed changed. I had grown. I had progressed.

I was on holiday and shared a table with women in their eighties and nineties, my parents' generation. I was able to see them more clearly than I had my parents. I was able to appreciate more just what this generation had been through and how they had prepared the way for my and future generations. I was able to understand more the hardships and deprivations that had influenced and fashioned my parents. These women were incredible people, full of life and wisdom, and yet often they were overlooked, no longer listened to… no longer even seen.

An Older Generation

>They went through the war.
>They grew up in times of scarcity.
>They knew what it was like not to be able to earn a living,
>So they worked hard and kept on working.
>They grew stoical and made do with what little they had.

They learned the need to look out for each other,
The last generation to fully appreciate the need for
    community.
They each played their part,
Hard-working, thrifty, uncomplaining,
Looking after their own, reliable and stable.

No teenage years to foster dreams,
They saw life as it was and accepted their place in it,

But they had hopes and an aim:
A better life for their children.
This is where their energies centred –
Not for themselves, but that their children
Would better themselves, would have it easier…
An unselfish wish.

We prospered as a result of their endeavours,
We took off and gained freedom
Because they provided a stable platform from which
    we could fly.

Do we appreciate this?
Do we look at them now and realise what they did for
    us,
Providing the springboard for our future?

Or do we just see the age
The bent, wrinkled, greying bodies?
Do we dismiss them as of no longer any account,
Fail to see the wisdom and growth behind the
    facades?

The ninety-year-old
Who finds people and places full of interest and wonder,

> The 'foreigner'
> Who views going down to breakfast as another
>   experience in life.
>
> They have learnt the secrets of living;
> They have the simple answers to the questions Youth
>   poses,
> But Youth forgets to ask them.
>
> But then, Youth has to learn these answers for itself;
> It does not work any other way.

I can see my mother and father so much more clearly now. I am able to view them with love and compassion. They were good people, honest and hard-working. My mother loved animals, taking in many a stray (I grew up with dogs, cats and goldfish). She had a generous heart under all the mood swings. She had a potentially outgoing, exuberant personality which had been straitjacketed first by her grandmother and then my father. Her wings had been clipped at a very early age. My father was a quiet man of integrity. He stood by his convictions. He was a staunch union man all his working life, the treasurer of his local branch attending meetings each week, until my mother spent some of the union money he had collected – she was not very good at eking out the small amount of housekeeping she received. He replaced it but he resigned from the position, I assume because he didn't want to be put in that position again. He would never walk through an official picket line, yet towards the end of his working life, when wildcat strikes (ones not having the official backing of the union) were sweeping the country, he was the only one to break the picket line at his works, as he considered there was no real reason for that particular downing of tools, plus the union had not sanctioned it. He was held in such respect that other men followed him and it all collapsed. I felt proud of him for that. Of course, he didn't tell me any of this but my mother faithfully relayed it all.

They championed the underdog. They took the farm worker,

Jimmy Flynn, under their wing, and he would often visit when I was young. I remember him in the house only when I was in my early teens, but earlier I remember my mother sitting on the steps outside the back door plucking a chicken he had brought from the farm or a sack of cabbages in the garage. Jimmy was a long way from his home in Ireland. When not working, he made his way to the local pub, drank hard and rolled home, swearing and cursing at all and sundry. My parents saw through this rough façade to the lonely, good-hearted man beneath. Whenever he visited he would ask me if I was playing wag, which meant was I skipping school. He was convinced I was. Always the same question; it was probably the only thing he could think of to say to me, and maybe it's what he used to do anyway. He bought me an Easter egg each year, usually frosted sugar ones. When I was about fifteen the farmer sold his fields to a developer and they were left unworked for many years. Having spent his life outdoors, Jimmy ended up in a factory. I heard he started 'walking out' with the single mum with the hunchback brother. I thought that was good – two lonely people, both shunned by the people around them, getting together. Tragically, he died of pneumonia within six months of leaving the farm. I can empathise with the loneliness. There were and are so many lonely people around, yet being physically on one's own does not necessarily mean loneliness. I have never lived on my own, and yet a large part of my life I have been crippled with a sense of loneliness. I realise now that when I am feeling like this my sacral chakra is out of balance, the one that provides us with the ability to reach out and relate to people, to feel connected to others.

My parents would have helped me like a shot if it was in their means and had I asked. One time I remember sitting in their house with my three-month-old daughter on my knee and worrying about what we were going to do about money after my husband had had his motor racing accident. The race track had been in nearby Cheshire, so I was able to stay with my parents. We relied for money on my husband working all hours in his business. My father offered to lend us his savings. He didn't have much, but they would have given us anything in that moment to make it better. I refused but appreciated the offer. Fortunately, my husband was not as severely injured as feared, and was out of hospital in a week.

I see now how my parents shared a sense of working-class inferiority, exacerbated by a crippling lack of confidence. They were from a generation that had well-defined roles of how a man and his wife should live. This may have suited my father to some extent, but my mother must have chafed under the restrictions to her more outgoing personality. Although from the anger my father carried perhaps they both did – my uncertainty arises from the fact that I knew my mother better than my father.

They tried to do what they saw as their duty as best they could. Nursing my great-grandmother could not have been easy, and for several of those years they had my father's elderly father living with us as well. I think my mother felt she was even more of a drudge during those years and resented it bitterly. Money was tight, but within their means they provided for me, although at the time I was not always as grateful as I could have been. I realise that they did the best that they could and that they had loved me as much as they were capable. They would have been devastated to think that they were damaging me in any way or causing me unhappiness. They really were decent people. As Marilyn Monroe once said about her childhood, 'It wasn't really that bad, I just took it hard.' Me too.

For many years after my mother's death I wished I could have been more appreciative while they were still alive, instead of fearfully keeping my distance. In emergencies I was there, but from day to day I stayed apart. I know they were disappointed in me because I was not there for them as much as they thought I should be, even changing their wills at one point to express their displeasure (later torn up). I wished that I had had the awareness I have now so that I could have responded differently to them, been more understanding of their own unhappy childhoods and restrictive lives, more sympathetic to the burdens they shouldered.

Yet, as I become more aware, these feelings are dissipating. I understand now that we played our parts perfectly for the experiences we all needed, and I thank them, beautiful souls that they are, for journeying with me along my path.

Accepting I am now perceived as part of the older generation, I look around me with increasing equanimity. I can look back down that long path I travelled on and see it with a clarity and an understanding that I didn't have when I was in the midst of that part of my journey. Each step I took brought me nearer to awakening, each experience increased my awareness, my self-realisation – no matter that many of those steps were taken in darkness. I am also able to see those around me more clearly, including my children, to see them as the beautiful souls they are in this human experience.

MOTHER'S DAY

Tomorrow I see my children
And I marvel at *who* they have become.

Out of my womb they emerged,
Struggling and squalling,
Two unique human beings
Ready to take on the challenge
Of growing and experiencing.

Laughing and crying,
Happy and sad,
Loving and hating,
Hurting and hurtful.

And they now stand before me,
Tall and true,
Shaped and tempered,
Their soul-goodness shining forth
Even when surrounded
By the blocks and protections of their humanity.

I honour you both and am privileged
To have been part of your process,
As you journey towards the Light.

Remembering Those I Met Along the Way

Over the years I have met and connected to many different people but can no longer remember their names. Yet the names of the children I grew up with during those first ten years are as vivid in my memory as ever. I am going to list them here. Feel free to skip over them; they are of interest only to me, but I want to pay tribute to the times we spent together during our summer idylls. David and Rita, Susan and Carol, Dorothy, Annette, Leon and Michael, Keith, Lilian and Christine, Larry and Valerie with her five older siblings. I spent a lot of time with the sisters Susan and Carol. Once I remember Susan falling out with me and calling me bossy. Projection starts at a very young age – she was the one who liked to be in charge of us all. I played a lot with David and spent a lot of time in their house. We started school together. Sadly, his younger sister, Rita, died at the age of nineteen. They have all left me with good memories. Oh, there were the times when my mother would fall out with Leon and Michael's mother, and we children were not allowed to talk to each other until they made up – and we didn't – but even that sort of memory means that for those few years I felt part of the community. That feeling disappeared in my teens and did not return.

It was not until after I had my children that I started to make friends again. Initially, perhaps, it was because I could hide behind my children until I learned to trust and relax. Wanting my children to have a very different experience to mine, I began to seek out other mothers, ostensibly for the children to play together but also for me to begin sharing and connecting to like-minded people. We would talk, share, laugh and cry together, supporting each other. There were many names in those young children years but the ones that have stayed in my memory are Pat, Sally, Mair and Penny. Communication became essential to me. Communication is one of my life lessons, hence the initial experience of being unable to communicate (my childhood years) and then beginning the process of learning how to communicate at all the different levels there are. During these first years it was at the level of exchanging ideas and beliefs. It was 'I think' rather than 'I feel'. Sometimes I would be so immersed in the experience that I would forget everything around, as when visiting Mair when we realised suddenly that we could not hear the children. We rushed into the kitchen to find they had climbed on to the unit top to search the cupboards for sweets, and were just in the process of opening a bottle of orange sweeties – junior aspirin! That was a near miss, but oh, the guilt! Or again with Sally, sitting in the garden on a summer's day, so absorbed in the conversation we forgot the time and I was late collecting my daughter from primary school.

Around this time, there was one small, practical helping hand that I received from Sally. I had travelled the 200 miles to my parents in my Mini with my two very small children and all their paraphernalia. I was to collect my mother from a day's stay in hospital as her responsible adult. My mother phoned to say the hospital were keeping her in to do an emergency hysterectomy and she would be there for two weeks. My father could not be left on his own for long, as he had had a stroke and walked only with the aid of a frame. I could not fit him in to my car with the children, their stuff and his frame. I phoned my husband to come in his larger car, only to find he had hurt his back and needed to lie flat for a few days. Consequently, I took the children home there and then and the next day did the round trip again with my father and his belongings. While I was doing this Sally arrived with a huge casserole enough to feed everyone for a couple of days – just the right thing. I've never forgotten that. The picture is a clear as if it was yesterday and it was over thirty-five years ago. Helping hands come in all guises.

There were friendships that lasted only while we were sharing painful episodes in our lives but which could not be sustained today. I supported A through her periods of schizophrenic breakdown. At this time of my life, not only was I depressed and could resonate at that dark level but also I had the need to be needed. This relationship fulfilled that need, as many of A's friends withdrew when they first experienced her paranoia. Years later, I could no longer be leaned on in this way. Rather than empathising with that dark, despairing energy, it now felt too raw and draining. It is as though my energy recoils from it. Later, when the friendships were no longer child-oriented, I remember C and J. Although for a few years C and I united over the difficult relationships we had with our mothers, I could no longer sustain this relationship when I made my peace with my mother and let go of all the negative feelings surrounding her. There was no common ground any longer as C was still stuck in her codependent relationship with her mother.

J and I shared the anger, pain and turmoil of our marriages breaking down. Also I supported her through her first nervous breakdown. When it occurred again five years later, I could not be there for her. Empathising with someone else's dark night of the soul no longer resonated because I was starting to come out of my own. There was also the feeling that the experiences we have are to be learned from. I felt impatient that she had continued with exactly the same behaviour that had contributed to the first one. (Two of my traits which were still quite strong during this period and as yet I had not started work on – judgment and impatience!)

Anne came into my life as I was going through my divorce. She was particularly supportive at that time and continued to be so over the years. She died a few years ago and I wrote this in her memory. I am still in touch with her husband, Michael.

To Anne

My heart is filled with such fond memories
Of times when we connected,
Two souls meeting and remembering.

You were always more than you ever thought you were.
Your spirit shone through in a world of turmoil and darkness,
A beacon of light for all those troubled souls
Who were stumbling through life,
And who sheltered for a while
In the embrace of your love and compassion.

> Even though you suffered such emotional roller-coaster rides,
> So often doubting, feeling crushed and hopeless,
> Unable to see your true worth,
> You still reached out to others, sensing their need, feeling their pain,
> A beacon of light for those locked in a world of misery and confusion.
>
> And you comforted and soothed, you encouraged and reassured
> Until hope sprang from despair and smiles replaced tears.
> And I thank you for being there in my times of turmoil and despair,
> A listening ear, a reaffirming word, a loving embrace – a friend.
>
> And I thank you also, Michael,
> For your kindness, your keen mind, your sound advice,
> And for being the steady rock for Anne to lean on,
> Providing her with the stable foundation
> From which she was able to shine her light into the world.

I have worked in many places. I was told years later that I was meant to work in many places as this would enable me to experience relating to many different people and that if I did not move on, then the Universe would ensure that I did. It became clear that this was the case. When I was younger I had no worries about leaving a job and did so regularly. As I got older, I found change more difficult, as I was getting in touch with my feelings, which included my fear of the unknown. When I refused to move on, no matter how uncomfortable the workplace was becoming, the job would change around me. For example, a favourite boss would leave and my whole job and circle of co-workers would change as I was moved to work for someone else; or I would be forced to move on as when they sent my boss to prison and the office was closed down.

In all I have had twenty-two employers (I can be very detailed!), and some of those were temporary agencies, which means I have met and connected (or not) with many people along the way. Some of those connections have been joyous, some have been very uncomfortable, yet all were the very experience I needed at the time.

LEAVING WORK

A lovely day,
Sun shining
Inside and out.

People approaching
With good wishes in their hearts,
A time to express thanks
And appreciation for each other,
To hope for good times in the future,
To honour the time spent together.

No looking back
But a warm acknowledgment
Of the blessings received
From having walked side by side
For this short while.

From the 1960s I remember Imelda and June. I was moving quite rapidly from job to job in those days, but these two stand out, the one in Manchester the other in London. I remember the energetic flow between Imelda and me. It was a revelation that people could connect in this way. I had not experienced it before. Later, in London I worked with June for a while before she left to go to America. She was older than me and I appreciated her down-to-earth wisdom. I recall other faces too but the names have long gone.

In the 1970s, I was bringing up children and bookkeeping for my husband's engineering business until separation took me back out to work in a family social work unit, where I met Robin, L and J. For a few years we shared closely in each other's lives, from the winter L and J came for baths when they were having a very old house renovated, through the pain of stillbirth, to the joy of their further two children. Robin is multi-talented, a musician, writer, with an affinity with the eighteenth century – a true eccentric, walking his own path rather than society's. We correspond in the old-fashioned way, not quite like *Ladies of Letters*, but sufficient that we remain part of each other's lives so that occasionally we meet up and renew our connection. Grace, Maureen and I meet regularly ever since we watched and worried while our boss was arrested, tried and convicted in the 1980s.

In the 1990s I worked for a short time with Hannah, Julie and Sandra at the local council's housing department. Hannah and I shared an interest in metaphysics. There was an instant connection and we had many wonderful discussions. Julie, Sandra and I still meet from time to time, mainly thanks to Julie who takes care of all those around her. I appreciate Julie's insight and Sandra's wisdom and the fact that both of them value friendship.

There have been numerous others whose company I have enjoyed, whose problems I have listened to, as they have mine, who have included me in their joys and shared with me the pain of their losses. So many people, so many souls touching and connecting for that short moment. It has been a privilege to meet and connect with all these people.

Meeting Together

> We meet together, you and I,
> To share our journey and to raise our energies,
> So that when we are ready we will go forth recharged
> To spread the seeds of change and to lighten the dark
>   corners.

> At times we get stuck and we feel disconnected and
>   alone
> And so we meet together, you and I,
> To help each other reconnect and
> To open ourselves again to the Light.

This was the way I learned, through the direct experience of every day life and relationships. Sometimes the experiences were warm and comforting, sometimes very difficult and unpleasant. This was how I grew and developed.

As well as the different work environments, I have also belonged to many and varied groups, some social, some with a purpose, again meeting and relating to many different people. I would walk with them for a few years and then, as our paths went in different directions, new people would come into my life to accompany me. There were evening classes (from French to social psychology, bookkeeping to comparative religions), babysitting circles, National Housewives' Register, book and theatre groups, bridge playing, women's sexuality, Rights of Women, women's consciousness raising, assertiveness training, self-awareness groups, meditation groups, ascension groups, even a group for giving up smoking followed by Weightwatchers! I am still in touch with Marie and Carol from the time when we were volunteer Samaritans nearly thirty years ago. I met Joyce through the 'stress and self-awareness' course I took in 1987 that started me on my spiritual explorations. Eventually she reached the conclusion that it was not stress she was experiencing but distress. Ever since I have known her she 'never achieves the tasks I intend to do each day', as she puts it. A lovely, big-hearted person, she does a lot for others in spite of her own distressful home life.

I learned to become aware of how I was feeling and acting when in any group, as this can be a strong reflection of our primary group (the family group we grew up in). I am what is known as a 'boundary person' because I tend to stay on the edge of a group rather than jumping into the centre. Some will immediately feel more comfortable being in the centre of a group, the focal point of the group's attention, and there are varying degrees in between. Wherever we find ourselves is probably where we were when we were growing up. There is no right or wrong place to be. For many years when I was in a group, especially new ones full of 'strangers', I felt isolated, uncomfortable and ill at ease, thinking I should and wishing I could be in the centre. Such feelings came from my childhood years, and I was re-experiencing them so that eventually they could be worked through and released. Now I am quite comfortable in my boundary position. If I need to, it is no longer a problem to draw attention to myself and express my truth, but I have no problem letting others take centre stage. I recognise that for any group to fulfil its purpose, it needs both its centre and boundary positions to be filled. We all have our part to play within it and all are of equal importance. The talkers need listeners, the listeners need talkers; the ebullient need an audience, the audience needs its players.

Throughout my journey there have been many moments of loneliness and disconnection, but in later years I would be incredibly uplifted when I met and connected with other kindred spirits. Often it would be in a group or workshop and then the brief encounter would be over and we each went our different way. However, some of these beautiful souls remained in my life for a while and we walked the path side by side, sharing, understanding, supporting each other – blessed companions. Many such encounters were in the many personal and spiritual development courses I began doing after the Harmonic Convergence. Among others, I did some fascinating courses at the College of Psychic Studies and the School of the Living Light.

GATHERING TOGETHER

We gather together, a meeting of kindred spirits
To share in the wonder that the spiritual path brings

A celebration of our journey, each one unique
As we search through the darkness for a way back to
   the Light,

> A moment of respite when we once more connect
> With the love and wisdom that surrounds and protects.
>
> Together our Souls sing a song of love
> That reaches out toward the Light
> And in that moment the Universe stills
> And for that moment we remember Who We Really Are.

During my two years of counsellor training, I connected deeply with Alex, Kamiljit and yet another Anne. (There have been a lot of Annes and Annas in my life!) There was also the Anne who ran the course. Her help was invaluable. I respected and admired her and learned so much from her. I connected also with Anna and Helen, both of whom have continued to walk with me. I feel very wise and very present when I meet with Anna, a reflection of her energy. She has travelled the globe and is very at home in the cultural diversity of London – I call her my 'cosmopolitan friend'.

It was also during this course that I learned that I was not expected to like everyone. I was not necessarily being intolerant or lacking in some way if I was unable to do so. It was more that maybe they have personality traits that don't resonate with my traits. It was a relief to learn that it was a waste of my energy trying to get through to someone when it was obvious they couldn't 'hear' me, and that it was better to accept it wasn't going to happen and move on. We are all different; we have each brought with us our own unique script for this lifetime. We are none of us here to live up to expectations of each other. As Fritz Perls says in his Gestalt Prayer: *I am I and you are you. If by chance we meet, it's beautiful. If not, it can't be helped.*

This understanding made a big impact on me. Before this I had been beating myself up at not being able to make these connections. The trick, though, is to realise that whatever the barrier is, it stems only from our personality traits. Even if we don't 'meet' everyone, because we don't like their behaviour or we cannot connect with them in any meaningful way, we can still remember who they really are even as we pass on – eternal souls, just as we are.

After the counselling group, there followed light body and ascension courses. Emma is a highly aware soul who enlightens all who connect with her. Suzi has an artist's eye and highlights the beauty and harmony to be found in colour. Gwen has a fey sensitivity, and Catherine's energy is of will and power. Sarah is a dreamer whose light shines out no matter how deep her process. Lorraine's energy is wise and loving and the depth of connection between us inspired insights for both of us. I met Lynda, a very gentle and caring soul, walking in the woods, and we shared many an hour in rustic teashops. You can meet a Lightworker anywhere!

All of them carry a different energy yet each one is playing her part in the bigger picture. Although we may share certain traits with another, there is in fact no one who is exactly the same as you. Each of us is unique. Our energy signature is purely our own. I spent a large part of my life *trying to be like others*. Now I realise I can only be me, and finally that's OK because between us we highlight all the differing aspects of the Whole.

Friendships can last a lifetime but many are more short-lived. Such relationships have a natural end. You have received the message intended for you. You have learned what you needed to know. You have supported each other for the allotted time. However, often the personality does not understand the relationship has served its purpose, becomes attached and cannot let go. You may think you have let go, but if you still have uncomfortable feelings towards someone you used to know, then there is still an emotional attachment that needs to be released. Also, if you make a really deep connection with someone, it can feel hard to lose that connection if there is no similar one in your life at that time. Many Lightworkers have had moments of feeling isolated in this way. However, sometimes the old needs to leave our lives before the new can come in.

Of course, it is not always necessary to have to meet someone physically for them to have an affect on you. The following was written in 2002 in protest at the stoning of a woman in Nigeria for adultery. I thank the soul that was Amina, who played her part so wonderfully so as to enable us to unite in this manner.

SISTERHOOD

> Allying with women to support each other in common cause
> As we raise our voice in protest at the stoning of Amina,
> The energy of righteous anger, of compassionate protest
> The power of a common voice, the empowerment of belonging –
>
> I don't need physical presence to be part of a group, to feel part of a group,
> In this lifetime I am a woman, I belong to the World Sisterhood,
> I raise my voice, my energy to enhance that collective energy –
>
> We are one half of a whole, the energy of the masculine/feminine,
> The yin and the yang that creates the balance of the Whole,
>
> And when we finally raise our voice as one,
> When finally we raise our collective eyes, our whole focus to the Light,
> We become the Light once more connected to Source, to All That Is.

Another Lightworker I have never met but with whom I share my journey is Patricia, a beautiful, high-vibrating soul who lives in Portugal. We speak on the telephone from time to time, appreciating the beauty of having a kindred spirit to share with as we journey through this lifetime. Her way is very different from mine. For one thing she experiences the energies around far more physically than I do; for another her dreams are a very powerful part of her process, whereas I rarely remember mine. Yet synchronicities do occur, such as the day I was writing about coming into my power and she phoned to say that she had just undergone an intense experience to the extent that she felt she had come into her power.

Those who are walking closely with me today are Helen, Marie and my daughter, Makia. We are there for each other. We share with each other. The relationships now are interdependent rather than codependent. We each walk in our own space. We provide mutual support but there is no leaning. Helen has a depth of listening that is almost tangible. She is so present you know you are being heard, understood, even held in that moment. With Marie, when we phone each other, the first thing that happens is laughter. We laugh together. In the face of the latest challenge, we laugh. That is so uplifting. Makia (her soul name) has blossomed into a beautiful Lightworker with a high level of awareness. Another shining light. I am so grateful that they are in my life and this is for them.

FROM ME TO YOU

From me to you, a kindred spirit connecting and sharing
As we travel this road on a journey called life,

Reaching out to each other as we stumble onwards
Through the veils of illusion and the nights of despair

Until the going seems easier and the pace quickens
And our hopes raise as we glimpse the Light ahead.

Together we dance the last few steps of this our journey Home
And filled with love and peace and joy, we merge once more into the Light.

And, of course, my husband and my son, Ross. Both these souls share the same numerological numbers in this lifetime, and although neither is spiritually aware, they have an inner integrity, kindness, concern for others and sense of justice that is spiritual in its essence. After all, what is spirituality? To me *it's a way of being rather than a belief system.* My heart is full when I think of them. When I am preparing to meet up with my son I often use the words, 'I'm going to see my little boy.' He is thirty-eight years old, 6'2", shaven-headed, broad-shouldered, lean, athletic – and yet the picture of him in my mind is still the golden-haired four-year-old in his navy blue coat and red wellies.

Have you noticed I've given no names for my parents and husbands, from whom I have learned the most, who have been the most instrumental in my growth and development, and to whom I owe a large debt of gratitude? They were and are very private people. I honour that.

Not all my relationships were good and pleasant. Some I remember that caused me a lot of pain, and I'm sure I caused pain back. Although I would often wish to avoid these types of relationships, to retreat to my hermit cave and live in peace and quiet, I recognise that it is only through *all* types of relationships that I have been able to grow. The only way to discover what my strengths and weaknesses were was to be placed in situations that highlighted them. If I lived in a cave with no contact with the outside world, it might be relatively easy to believe myself to be the most calm and peaceful person in the world. But if I leave my cave and make my way down the mountain into the marketplace, I soon find that I carry irritation and impatience because other people keep getting in my way or behaving negatively towards me. It is only through the interaction with others that we experience these different aspects of ourselves and learn what is within us. I get up early each morning and peacefully eat my breakfast, reading the paper, but it's not until my husband comes into the room that I know whether I am so deeply at peace that nothing can disturb it, or whether it's a fragile peace that can easily be disrupted by another's energy.

We shine our light in many different ways. I have met many Lightworkers along the way all here to give a helping hand to those awakening. Many of them work in the alternative professions as healers, channels, teachers, therapists – crystal this and angel that! I have also met the young doctor in the busy A&E of the local hospital who is one of the most empathic and sympathetic people I have ever met, with just a big, big heart. I have also met the waitress in the local Harvester restaurant who, despite hardship, is ever cheerful, good-hearted, friendly and makes you feel better just being around her. Her story rounds off my stay in Greater London. I used to go to this Harvester regularly over the years and got to talk to her. She had married late in life but after two years (and after she had transferred her house into his name) her husband left her and sold everything over her head. Instead of retiring she had to continue working.

For about ten years I didn't go to this Harvester until just before my move last year when Grace, Maureen and I returned there one final time. The first person I saw was this waitress. She still had the same cheerfulness, nimble-footed movements and down-to-earth good humour. She said this was her final year too as she was retiring at the New Year, when she would be eighty! Plus, she still intended to keep her hand in the occasional cover at conventions and parties – she wasn't going to stop completely! As I say, we shine our light in many different ways.

OPENING TO THE LIGHT

Opening up to the Light that emanates from Source, like the unfurling petals of a flower, I am filled with joy and wonder. By the early 2000s I was writing using high, positive words – soul words. They possess an energy that refreshes the body, calms the emotions, clears the mind and uplifts the spirit. They inspire and excite, piercing through the heaviness of this planet's dense energy, lightening the energy around and within.

INTO THE LIGHT

The sun is in the heavens, shining on me,
Filling me with its warmth and light.

Sunlit green fields stretch before me
With birds singing and angels dancing.

> I look around, the journey is no more
> The mists of time were but an illusion.
>
> The angels of light beckon me and
> I run towards them into the Light.

When I talk of Light with a capital 'L' I am referring to Cosmic Light as opposed to sunlight. Another word for light is *energy*. Everything around us is energy, from high, fast-moving frequencies to low, dense vibrations. We are all energy. Thoughts, feelings and emotions are energy. There are different ways of experiencing energy. Many healers can actually feel energy as they channel it. Others sense it. Now my third eye is much more open, there are times when I see it.

In a workshop a couple of years ago, opening my eyes after a meditation where we had called upon the ascended masters, guides and angels to be present and we had reached a state of profound love and peace, the room was filled with Light. It was so bright. After a while my vision returned to normal and the light in the room returned to normal. If I want to check if something is right for me I visualise it in my mind's eye. If it looks light, then it is right for me. If it looks dark, then it isn't.

I visited a friend who had had to move after her mother died. They had been living together and had been very codependent. I walked into her new living room and my immediate impression was that it looked very dark and grey. The word 'mausoleum' flashed into my third eye. After a while my vision returned to normal and the room lightened. Yet the energy I had 'seen' was that of the darkness of depression and unhappiness and the room was filled to overflowing with her mother's belongings. My friend could not let go.

Another time in the counsellor training group, I was sitting in between two women who began shouting and screaming at each other. I shut my eyes and cringed away but the wall was behind me preventing me physically moving. I think then my mind must have backed away because suddenly I was 'seeing' each scream as bolts of lightning shooting across from the one to the other and back again. This has brought home to me how much powerful energy we each contain. If you ever feel or voice your anger at someone (even if they are not present), you are literally throwing it at them, just as I threw my clock all those years ago. I missed my target with the clock, but your feelings, thoughts and words never miss. This is why each of us needs to release such negativity and embrace all that is positive within us and around us. The more we open to the light of positive energy, the more we bring that light down to earth, lifting the darkness of misery or hatred that much of humanity still lives in.

All that we know on Earth is energy, all that is within us is energy, all that we aspire to is energy. And this energy is multi-hued and varied. It has qualities and vibrations that ripple through us and over us, from the whisper of the breeze, to the feeling of happiness, to the roar of a crowd. What of the calm, cool energy of the Moon, subtle and feminine? Or the vibrant warm energy of the Sun, dynamic and masculine? Or the clear radiant energy of a Star, translucent and transcendent? Reach out and touch these differing energies, see them, feel them, sense them, play with them – open to them.

Open to the Light

Open your eyes, your ears, your senses
To the realms of the soul,
To the higher realms of the Universe,

You will hear the joy of angels and
Resonate to the song of the Universe,
You will see the radiance of the Light
And feel it caressing you, blessing you.

Open to the Light,
See yourself,
Believe yourself,
You are the Light.

The very first spiritual awareness class I attended I learned about chakras and the importance of colour. Before then I would wear mostly black, occasionally red; but black is no colour, a complete lack of colour, which does not allow any positive energies to penetrate through. When the light emanating from Source reaches the Earth, it is made up of the colours of the spectrum that we see when a rainbow forms. Colour is energy, vibrating at different speeds depending on the colour. We need all these colours to remain balanced. It could be said that colour is a spiritual food. I am now very attracted to green, the heart chakra colour of calm, balance and love. With the extremes of mood that I was subjected to by my mother and was subject to myself, it makes sense to me that I need to wear green a lot for its balancing effect. It's not a conscious choice. If I'm looking for clothes, it's the green ones that attract me – they are the only ones I see. Recently, however, I have been drawn to white, and in my house I can no longer have dark coloured furniture around me. I prefer now to be surrounded by creams, whites and pastels rather than the brighter, richer or darker colours. Again, this is just for me for where I am at the moment. Maybe a vibrant colour is exactly what you need. Your energy is different, it's unique to you. Allow yourself to be drawn to a colour. Follow your own inner knowing.

At this class I heard the following guided visualisation – in fact it was one of the first I ever did. I don't recall what the wording was but I remember the image I had of each room, and it has remained with me as somewhere comforting and transforming to go to when I was in need of rebalancing. My words below give an outline of the images I have retained but they don't flesh out the detail; those remain in my inner house. It can be become whatever you want it to be – your own special house in which to curl up, to find peace, to regroup and find yourself, to reconnect with your spiritual essence. The idea is to start at the bottom of the house and climb stairs to each one until you reach the top.

THE RAINBOW HOUSE

The red hall is bathed in ruby-red light.
The floor is patterned with rubies and red crystals –
Draw the red energy through the soles of your feet
Your physical body resonating to its red vibration.
Absorb the vitality this red ray brings and begin to feel
  recharged.
Enhancing your physical vitality, your sense of being.

In the centre of the orange room is an apricot sofa –
Lie back among the peach-coloured cushions
Rest and relax as the orange ray seeps into you.
Absorb its warm expansive vibration,
Stimulating, it uplifts your spirits,
Enhancing your sense of enthusiasm and optimism.

In the yellow room, there's a pine floor
And bright yellow bookshelves filled with books –
Feel your energy becoming receptive to knowledge.
Golden sunlight is pouring in through the oval windows.
Breathe in this bright sunlit yellow ray,
Its light vibration increasing your confidence and
    personal power.

The green room is a conservatory filled with plants,
From fragile fern to shiny-leafed rhododendron
Light dances through the glass bathing you in an
    emerald green ray –
Feel your heart drawing in this soothing balanced
    vibration.
Absorb this healing ray of harmony and compassion.

The blue room has a pool and its sparkling blue water
Reflects the azure blue of the sky outside –
Float in the pool, the water gently caressing your skin
Enjoy the cleansing quality of this clear light blue ray,
Opening your expression of truth and creativity.

In the indigo room, with its deep blue velvet curtains
    and thick-piled carpet,
An open fire burns in the fireplace, warming and
    comforting
Through the window the stars shine in the midnight-
    blue sky –
Absorb the uplifting vibration of this cool indigo ray
Expanding spiritual awareness and intuitive knowing.

> In the violet room at the top of your house,
> The walls are covered in violet silk and the floor is amethyst
> Through the dome glass ceiling the sky is violet –
> Feel this spiritual violet/purple ray
> Absorb this transforming, enlightening vibration,
> Connecting you to your soul and higher dimensions.

When I 'see' the Light, it is mostly a very bright white – white, of course, is made up of all the colours of the rainbow. The Light coming in now is changing. The more positive we become, the more Light we absorb. The more we increase our own and the Earth's vibration, the more we can accommodate a higher frequency of Cosmic Light. The aim is for us all individually and as a whole, Mother Earth herself included, to move into the Fifth Dimension. These newer, higher frequencies of Light reaching us are apparently more pearlescent than third dimensional colours, more crystalline. They are fifth dimensional energies that at long last we are about ready to absorb. A few years ago they would have been too overwhelming.

LET THE LIGHT SHINE THROUGH

> Let the Light shine through
> Multicoloured hues and opalescent tints.
>
> Revel in its glorious divinity
> Imbued with the energy of clarity and truth.
>
> Take in this light with all its glorious potential,
> Let the crystal colours flow through you.
>
> Channel the delicate and breathtaking beauty
> That emanates from the Soul of Souls.
>
> Release these fifth dimensional harmonies
> To shine through the veil of humanity's vision,

> Sowing jewelled seeds of beauty and wisdom,
> Inspiring, exciting, uplifting.

Another word for the process of opening up to the Light is *ascension* (or as the Buddhists would call it, enlightenment). As I understand it, ascension is the process whereby we become self-realised first at the personality level, then at the soul level and then the monadic level – all while we are still in physical form. (Your monad is your soul's soul. It is the spiritual spark that has emanated direct from Source.) In other words the more we lighten our vessels (bodies) the more we can bring the higher vibrations of Light down into us and so on to the Earth.

When you become self-realised at the soul level, then you encompass the soul qualities of inner peace and calm, balance and harmony, joy and wonder, love and forgiveness, compassion with detachment, will and power, intelligence and discernment, trust, gratitude, humility and a sense of connectedness. Your soul is a being of light and love. It has a pure and radiant vibration, and when you rise up to the Soul Plane to merge with your soul, there is a sense of its vastness. You feel in that moment that you encompass star systems, span galaxies. This is who you really are.

We lighten ourselves on all levels, not just spiritually but also psychologically (mentally and emotionally) and physically. It means changing all that is negative into the positive. It means bringing all that is hidden into the light. We get to replay our processes (our issues or lessons) over and over again until we have released all our karma and childhood blockages, until we have reached our potential in this lifetime. We get to realise that Heaven is in fact where we are now. We get to realise that we are the Light.

According to Buddha there are four ways to enlightenment – quick and easy, quick and difficult, slow and easy or slow and difficult, or some such wording. Mine appears to be the slow and difficult. I seem to feel and experience with a great intensity so that it appears to be a struggle to get through my process, that is, my journey of self-discovery. I know that there is really no struggle; it just feels that way because my struggle is mainly with myself as sometimes I forget that it's OK to be me, that whatever I am feeling, whoever I am in any given moment, is OK. I have a tendency to beat myself up if I fall below my idea of what an aware spiritual person should be. Once I can accept that maybe I still have down days, can still lose my patience, still lack trust, then these feelings will lose their hold on me and I am free to move on.

The process I went through when I was doing my counsellor training course was intense and at times extreme. When it was all over I thought, Phew, thank goodness it's all over and I never have to go through that again! However, the move out of London turned into another intense process for me. All right, not as extreme as before, but the emotions coming up during the eighteen months between the decision to move and the actual move were at times strong and exhausting. The difference this time was that I was aware of what was happening, could understand it, and because of this I could contain it much more easily. My aware self was watching it all – with interest.

Many issues came up surrounding whether I had the right to assert my needs, not least when they were in direct opposition to another's. There is a phrase I have caught myself saying many times before: 'My heart went out to…' On this occasion, I remember sitting in front of my computer and thinking about my husband's need to stay put. How on earth could he move? He would feel this, he would miss that. I went into a warm, fuzzy, heart-rending, loving space as I thought of his situation – as my heart went out to him. Then I seemed to step back inside of me to a cool, calm, detached space that is the centre of me, and I realised I had been allowing myself to be overwhelmed with empathy and compassion. In that moment I realised I was doing again exactly what I did with my mother – giving my power away, allowing my empathy to overwhelm me, allowing someone else's needs to blot out my own. I was replaying my childhood (yet again), although with a newer and higher level of awareness.

Another issue was that I wanted to live in the countryside whereas my husband wanted to be in the town. How could we reconcile this? I felt my inner child's frustration and despair when she cried out once again 'Can I never have what I want?' There then followed that old feeling as my inner child started to collapse within: *It's too much effort – sink back into lethargy – just give up*. Then one day I had a moment of clarity that was so bright, so light, so simple and serene, it almost took my breath away. In that moment

I realised I could have anything I wanted. It was OK to assert my needs. I didn't need anyone else's approval or permission. It was a moment of perfect certainty, not just at the mental level but at all levels of my being. I felt such a sense of freedom – I was once more in my power, calm, confident and totally centred. Coming to that place of knowing, I found then that it was easy to compromise. Any decision I made now was based on free choice rather than a 'can't' or a 'should'. We live now in a place that is a mile from the town centre but very near open countryside.

Throughout it all were the tests for me of trust and patience. Trust that it would all happen perfectly and it did. At a time when the housing market was collapsing, we were still able to move. 'Oh, you are lucky,' everyone said. Not luck, rather trust in the outcome, trust in the bigger picture; patience that it would happen in its own time, and it did. In spite of my inner struggles it unfolded seamlessly.

One by-product of my move was the severing of a friendship. The culmination of the eighteen-month process was the move itself, which was a process in itself bringing up all sorts of emotional upheaval. When we moved I became very focused on arranging it all, carrying it out and at the same time supporting my husband. My mind was working overtime. It was a huge upheaval for us both, as neither of us change easily, my husband even less easily than I. It meant getting rid of a lot of old stuff because it held old energy (bear in mind my husband is a hoarder and never throws anything away!). It meant uprooting ourselves, which brought up a lot of fear and, once we were in the new place, trying to find our feet without slipping (we were very wobbly for a while!). So, for a few weeks this was my whole focus, until I became physically, mentally and emotionally exhausted, to the extent that my physical body collapsed on me and I came to a full stop. The same pattern as previously – a period of intense personal change and then collapse in an exhausted heap. (This time it was only a few days, but I recognised the similarities and realised I needed to rest and recover.)

During this period I received an email from my friend Helen saying it felt like I was no longer there. I realised then that I had no energy reserves left, I was running on empty. This meant I had no energy to be there for anyone else and, of course, the uprooting itself had also contributed to this disconnection. Helen was OK about it because she is very aware; however, another friend, feeling this disconnection, reacted to it personally and felt rejected. She withdrew, and when I was back on balance again (it didn't take as long as last time to recover) I sensed the withdrawal and was puzzled by it. I tried to reach out tentatively but she had withdrawn from the relationship.

It wasn't until later that I put the pieces together. An addictive personality, she had been leaning on me, and when I was no longer there energetically, she found herself falling. It had been a codependent relationship rather than an interdependent one. It brought home to me that a part of me still needed to be needed. I had replayed my role with my mother, listening and supporting, albeit at a much diluted level.

I sit writing this in my new room in my new house (all right, I know it's ours but 'my' seems more poetic!), and I look out the windows at the sun on the garden and I have a deep feeling of contentment. The above eighteen-month process is over and I've come out the other side. I'm not saying 'never again', though – I've learned my lesson. However, this time I was much more aware about what was happening and this helped me through it and, in all honesty, it was not that I couldn't or didn't cope. I understand that we are never given more than we are capable of coping with. It's only the personality that thinks it's too hard, and there is a part of me that can be very lazy, just wanting to be comfortable, meandering along and not making much effort. At the soul level it was time to face these issues. We replay and revisit these patterns and beliefs over and over until we have released them or found the positive in them, until we stand in our own true light.

Next time around it will be at a different level again. My awareness will be hopefully even more advanced, and maybe it will have seeped even more into my subconscious that it need not be a struggle, that I can let go into the flow of it. The greater the trust, the easier the ascension – the easier the journey into the Light.

May love, light and joy be your travelling companions as you continue your own journey into the Light.

Soul-presence on Earth

My first twenty years were in Lancashire. My next forty years or so were in Greater London. Now we have moved to Berkshire and it feels as though I have come full circle. Growing up, I could either walk the roads or go through the fields to reach the village. I have the same choice here. I have walked a few times through the fields into the small town, and each time it has begun with the walk down a narrow pathway in the middle of two ploughed fields, both of which have a crop just coming up, green tips sometimes silvered if it's frosty. Ahead the wintry sun has been out, low in the sky, and it feels just as though I am walking towards this big light and I have laughed with joy at this physical manifestation of our spiritual journey here. I am looking forward to the hawthorn blossom and the fresh green of the trees when spring comes in. If I walk the long way round, through woods and fields, over streams and rivers, I reach the lock and end up walking by the canal – just as in my childhood, although this canal is much smaller. No ocean-going liners here.

The Joys of Winter

Touching the smooth perfection of a snowdrop petal,
Seeing the blue in the sky when the grey clouds part,
Smelling the glistening pine on a wet afternoon,
Hearing the robin claiming its territory as the gardener works,
Tasting each warming morsel before it goes on to stoke our fires…

The joys of Winter on Planet Earth,
The benefits of being in physical form.

Touching the softness of a warming fleece,
Seeing the white snow as it magically transforms,
Smelling the wet hedgerows, stripped revealingly bare,
Hearing the depths in the silence when you stand in the field,
Tasting each soothing sip as it warms through to our toes…

>The joys of Winter on Planet Earth,
>The benefits of being in physical form.

The full circle feeling is also enhanced by people coming back into my life from childhood. I am still in touch with my school friend, Anne, whom I first met in the 1950s, and just recently I have heard from Valerie who lived in the same road as I did in the 1940s (apparently a couple of the mothers, now in their nineties, are still there!). She writes:

> To hear the name Jimmy Flynn was a real flash from the past as I remember him so well. He chased me many times for playing on the haystacks at harvest time.

We share the same memories. Full circle indeed! Having moved jobs and homes so many times, which often meant losing contact with many people, I find there are friends still in my life from nearly all the decades. This is a source of comfort. Instead of looking back down a long road, most of it lost in the mists of time, it feels as if it's been a circular journey. I have arrived back at those happy summer days of childhood, playing out in our pasture field, sharing and connecting with friends, carefree, living in the moment – but this time there's nothing hidden away, no black holes within.

IN THE SUN'S RAYS

In the sun's rays

I open to stillness
To the deep core within

And there find waiting
My forever self

In a sea of warm light,
In a field of serenity,

Wise and loving,
Filled with Grace,

The bliss to be found
In that moment of awareness

In the sun's rays.

We are indeed living in a new place – and not only geographically. Now that I am finding my balance again, it feels as though I am in a new place on all levels of being. It is as though I have suddenly cottoned on, at the most fundamental level, how to live and be while on Planet Earth. A trust is growing within me. I realise I have no need to strive or struggle to manifest; I need only wait for it to come to me. My soul is in the driving seat and knows what step to take next for my continued growth and development. This is for my type or design of person. I do understand that some people are wonderful manifestors who know exactly where they are going, but I am not one of them. I don't know consciously where I am going until I arrive there.

An example of this is the writing of these memories. I didn't set out to write a book. It evolved. It grew and kept on growing without any conscious planning from me. It has meandered along, rambled even, one moment a recent memory and the next a memory from childhood. Even now I don't know yet whether it's finished or not. I haven't started at the beginning and written it through to the end. I wake up each morning and another memory is there, and I add it in wherever it feels right for it to be. It has become a mishmash of the spiritual and the psychological, one moment reaching up to the Light and the next in the middle of a very earthly process. But maybe that is how my journey has been, a mishmash of the two, until one day they blend and it feels as if this is what is happening now. Because another realisation is that my purpose *is simply to experience*. I have awoken to the fact that it is a wonderful gift to be on Earth in physical form enjoying each and every experience given to me, even if those experiences are not so comfortable, because now my soul is fully present and aware of each moment.

SOUL-PRESENCE

I am sitting in a comfortable chair,
Eyes resting on the snow-covered lawn
Sparkling in the sunshine.
My mind is restless,
My feelings uncertain,
My body weary
And yet the I that I am
Is thoroughly enjoying this experience.

There is a joy within me,
Which does not stem from the state
Of my physical, emotional and mental bodies,
But yet could not be experienced without this physicality.
Notwithstanding the babble of my thoughts,
The churning of my emotions,
The niggles of my body,
There is a joy at being able
To see and touch, hear and smell
And to express my appreciation
Of this soul-present moment.

It is the joy in living,
Of being fully alive to each experience and
Of realising the underlying simplicity of it all.

Yes, I feel I have emerged into the light. I am no longer in a dark tunnel. I feel whole. I am far more aware. I feel alive. If I do have a 'down' day, then I know that it will pass, that it is not real.

No longer do I have a need to seek answers from others because I know that the answers are within me, or the Universe will provide them. No longer do I have a need to find out what new energies are coming in, what planetary influences are around, or what is humanity's collective mood, because all I have to do is check how I am feeling (although if you have trust issues, it is still heart-warming to have confirmation).

And so this memoir ends. This does not mean my journey has finished. I am still studying (at the moment with the I AM University). I still have a mind that at times goes into overdrive. When I started this writing and the memories were coming thick and fast, on a couple of occasions sleep was not possible until they were written. My self-discipline is still lacking sometimes when it comes to eating the wrong foods or not exercising enough. I can still feel impatience when my Taurus husband, a former lecturer, explains something three different ways (so his students would understand it better – he was a very fine lecturer), but I got it the first time and am now waiting for the punch line! I'm a Gemini; quicksilver-minded, we jump ahead. We want to be on to the next new idea. That's an explanation for my impatience, but it does not absolve me from improving my patience, from remembering to step into acceptance. Very occasionally, when I am overtired or overstressed, then the part of me that says 'I'm not good enough' will pop up and make its presence known. But I retain my awareness that this is just a part of me, an echo of a deep-seated belief that had enmeshed me for long years. A good night's sleep or a period of rest and I am back on balance.

We each have an affinity to a particular part of nature. Jean, a friend, after a lifetime in the city has just moved to be near the sea. Walking on the beach next to that mighty power source brings her into balance as nothing else can. The peace that lies within her emerges there. You might prefer sitting on a riverbank, mesmerised by the flow of water and the ever-widening ripples as fish rise to the surface. Or walking in the hills, breathing in the cleansing, fresh, clear air, with the sound of a sparkling stream cascading over moss-covered stones. At such times we reconnect to the Earth, tune into its life force, re-energise and re-ground.

For me, it is the countryside. If I am asked to visualise being in a place of beauty in nature, I find myself sitting in a field on a summer's day leaning back against a tree. Most of the places I have lived have overlooked fields or small wooded areas even if, in the middle of the city, they were only a school playing field or a golf course. (As with my jobs, I have also moved homes a lot.) And I have always, always, had a tree to look at. As a child I looked out at an old pear tree in the back garden and played with a dog on the small lawn in the front garden under the shade of three lilac trees, with a cat in one of them away from the dog. As I write this I can pause to look out at the trees that surround us now – beech and maple, willow and chestnut and many more. In my early years I didn't realise how important trees were to me, how much time I have spent gazing at them or leaning against them. I see trees as the guardians of the countryside, ambassadors for Mother Nature, and I absorb their calm strength, resonating to the earth wisdom that emanates from them. Time passes, but somehow they remain steadfast in the moment.

When I am in nature I find myself again; I come back to centre, re-energise, balance and ground. I wrote the following a few years ago but this is what I always go back to – these moments leaning against a tree on a summer's day, when just for a moment the universe seems to still and I find myself in this beautiful moment – this is my idea of Heaven on Earth.

RESTING FOR A MOMENT

A resting place,
A deep feeling of peace,
Contentment and calm,
An outer manifestation
Of the inner core of my being.

I travel along my path
Among the fields and trees;

The blue of the sky
And the green of the grass
Soothe my soul,
Calm my racing mind
And quieten my turmoil

My path stretches ahead of me
Into the golden sunlight

I rest awhile along my way
Against the strength of a tree
And I gaze around me
And feel the joy of living.

I listen to the song of the birds,
The rustle of the breeze in the trees,
The buzz of the bee winging by,

I watch the butterfly and dragonfly,
The movement of the leaves

And give thanks for being part of this moment
And for all the moments that have gone
And for all those to come.

I have still more levels of awareness to achieve and Light to absorb. Each day will bring more experiences, but there is no longer any fear as to what they might be. Instead there's anticipation, sometimes excitement, always hope, and a knowing that, even if uncomfortable, it's all happening perfectly.

I wish you sunlit days and soul-present moments.

Ann

Postscript: One Year Later

Looking back over the past year, it is clear that the process of writing down these memories was an act of completion. Although I didn't realise it at the time, it was summing up a way of living that has now ended; a tidying up of all the loose ends and drawing it to a close. It was an appreciative last look back before I stepped forward into the life I have now. I feel I am in a totally different space.

It's as though the world I inhabited over the past few years – very spiritual, meditative and removed – has been replaced by an explosion of colour and sound as I emerge as if from a chrysalis into this brand new dimension that we have moved into. From being surrounded by only white and pastels, I am now also attracted to bright vibrant colours. I am enjoying just *being* in this brand new physical world I find myself in, appreciating it to its full, delighting in every physical sensation.

Now I appreciate being surrounded by people, connecting into souls in all their various personality disguises and at an energetic level this connection can be achieved even if we are just passing the time of day. Really looking at someone while laughing about the weather is all that it takes. When seeing, acknowledging and honouring who they really are, then the words become unimportant. It's a moment of recognition. It's a moment of connection – connection at the soul level.

I want to share my love of being alive, to express my appreciation of the physical experiences we are all having. If I walk now, it is usually with others. I still need time on my own, but the balance between this and being with others is not as weighted as it once was.

The last few years have been difficult for us all as we were moving from one dimension to another. We were all affected in our own individual ways depending on what experiences we had created for ourselves and how our personalities were still programmed to react to them. But always, even in the midst of discomfort, there was the awareness that this was just yet another experience and that I no longer need to *do* anything to solve it or heal it. It was just a beautiful human experience. My mantra if I felt unrest was simply '*I am*' and I was back to centre.

I saw my first snowdrop the other day, a beautiful symbol of hope for the year stretching before us waiting for our imprint. I feel excitement. All those beautiful feelings and sensations to look forward to and the realisation that no matter what goes on around me deep within is a pool of calm and serenity, of total love and appreciation for Planet Earth and for the human experience I am having. My five senses have never been so precious to me, my sixth sense so enhanced. And I can write this even though yesterday I felt edgy, lethargic and muddled. It was just another passing experience, part of the rich diversity of feelings and sensations that being in a physical body gives to us.

At a soul level, we are all connected, a fact that we forget when we are born and we experience separation and fear. This connection is becoming more and more apparent as our heart chakras begin to re-open (helped along by those willing souls who depart in great numbers in the tsunamis, earthquakes or other such global experiences that touch us and in the touching change us). Don't you feel it? If you have been guided to read this, then your ascension process is well on its way, your soul connection and sense of presence stronger than ever. Stop and go within and there you will find your real self – that spark of awareness within that is watching all that you experience. Connect into its compassionate detachment and age-old wisdom. All your answers lie there. Whisper to yourself *I am* and in that moment you are the beautiful and unique soul that you really are.

Namaste